Dassault Rafale

France's Key to Air-Superiority

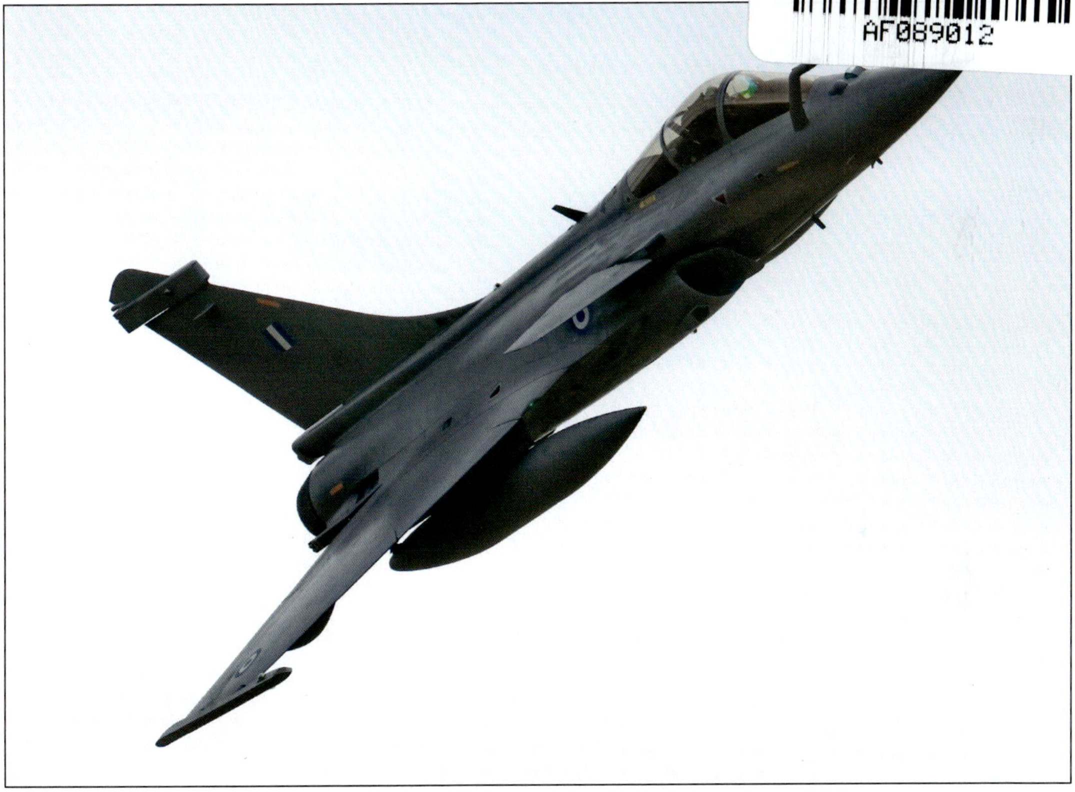

BABAK TAGHVAEE

KEY Books

MODERN MILITARY AIRCRAFT SERIES, VOLUME 13

Front cover image: When this Rafale B with s/n 325 was photographed on 15 October 2020, it was in use by the Escadron de Transformation Rafale 3/4 Aquitaine with 4-HX code at BA113 Saint-Dizier. In this image it is under control of the Rafale Solo Display team pilot and his instructor (back seat) during an airshow. (Babak Taghvaee)

Title page image: 411, a Rafale EG from the Hellenic Air Force is banking over Tanagra Air Base during the handover ceremony of the aircraft to 332 Mira on 19 January 2022. (Babak Taghvaee)

Contents page image: 328/104-IC, a Rafale B from the French Air Force's EC 3/30 'Lorraine', which was based in BA104 Abu-Dhabi until 2017. Together with a Rafale C from the same squadron, it was sent to LIMA 2015 airshow in Langkawi island, Malaysia, in March 2015. This Rafale B was later modified to carry ASMP-A nuclear cruise missiles and entered service with EC 1/4 Gascogne in BA113 Saint-Dizier. (Babak Taghvaee)

Back cover image: This Rafale M (Marine) with s/n 6, is one of 41 examples currently in use by the French Navy Aviation. It is armed with two MICA-EM BVRAAMs loaded under the wings and two MICA-IR ASRAAMs loaded on its wingtip launchers. (Babak Taghvaee)

Published by Key Books
An imprint of Key Publishing Ltd
PO Box 100
Stamford
Lincs PE9 1XQ

www.keypublishing.com

The right of Babak Taghvaee to be identified as the author of this book has been asserted in accordance with the Copyright, Designs and Patents Act 1988 Sections 77 and 78.

Copyright © Babak Taghvaee, 2023

ISBN 978 1 80282 591 6

All rights reserved. Reproduction in whole or in part in any form whatsoever or by any means is strictly prohibited without the prior permission of the Publisher.

Typeset by SJmagic DESIGN SERVICES, India.

Contents

Introduction 4

Chapter 1   The French Navy's Rafale Marines 9

Chapter 2   Rafale B/Cs of the French Air and Space Force 36

Chapter 3   Rafales of Egypt, Greece, India and Qatar 74

Introduction

Logging its first flight on 4 July 1986, Dassault Rafale is now the most advanced French-made fighter jet. It is in service with the armed forces of five countries. In February 2023, 245 Dassault Rafales in three types and 11 different sub-variants were airworthy. Among them, 90 were in service with the French Air and Space Force (FASF), 41 with the French Naval Aviation, 23 with the Egyptian Air Force, 12 with the Hellenic Air Force, 36 with the Indian Air Force and 36 with the Qatar Emiri Air Force.

The arrival of the first prototype Rafale A at Dassault's Aviation facility in Istres in 1985. (Dassault Aviation)

Introduction

In service with the French Naval Aviation (Navy) since 2001 and the FASF since 2003, the Rafale M (Marine) and Rafale B/Cs have proved their combat capabilities in several war theatres during multiple operations since 2007. From participation in the war against the Taliban and Al-Qaeda in Afghanistan, and beginning in 2014 the air war on ISIL/Daesh during Opération *Chammal* in Iraq and Syria, these aircraft proved to be the best air asset of the French armed forces against terrorism.

Since the Russian invasion of Ukraine began on 24 February 2022, the French Navy and then the FASF Rafales armed with MICA-IR, MICA-EM and Meteor air-to-air missiles have performed tens of combat air patrols over NATO's eastern front protecting its airspace and land territory.

The FASF Rafale Bs are equipped with ASMP-A nuclear cruise missiles have been in use for deterrence missions since 2010 enabling France to respond to any possible nuclear strike on any NATO member state in less than three hours.

Since 2015, the Rafale has proved to be a successful product in the multi-role fighter jet market. In the years between 2015 and 2023, Dassault Aviation delivered 102 brand new and six secondhand (refurbished) Rafales to four foreign customers, and is expected to deliver 164 more to two of them as well as two new customers by the mid-2030s.

France's success in selling these fighter jets to Asian and African customers is the result of four decades of work by Dassault Aviation and other companies involved in the design, development and production of the fighter jet; its M88-2 turbofan engines, RBE2 AESA radar, and other flight and mission systems; and also the result of the aircraft's successful operations in service with the French Navy and French Air and Space Force.

On 4 July 1986, Guy Mitaux-Maurouard, chief test pilot with the Rafale programme, took off for the first time with the Rafale A in Istres. (Dassault Aviation)

Left: On 4 July 1986, Guy Mitaux-Maurouard, chief test pilot for the Rafale programme, performed the maiden flight of Rafale A prototype at Istres. (Dassault Aviation)

Below: The Rafale A together with the team of its developers including the chief test pilot Jean-Frangois Cazaubiel, Guy Mitaux-Maurouard, Serge Dassault, Bruno Revellin-Falcoz, Charles Edelstenne. (Dassault Aviation)

The first Rafale A prototype logged its last flight in January 1994. During its eight-year-long flying career, the aircraft had 867 test flights performed by 30 different Dassault Aviation test pilots, among them 12 were from the Air Force and six were from the Navy. (Katsuhiko Tokunaga)

On 19 May 1991, the first production prototype of Rafale, numbered C01, logged its first flight and took the place of the Rafale A in flight test programmes at Istres. The aircraft was the star of many air shows and exhibitions until its retirement. It was then put in storage at Châteaudun Air Base in southwest Paris until 2019 when it was refurbished, repainted and displayed at the headquarters of the French Ministry of Defence. (Eric Bannwarth)

The prototype of the Dassault Rafale B (B01) during the Dubai Airshow in November 1995. In 2013, this prototype was transferred from Istres to Bruz to pass ground tests at the Directorate General of Armaments' (DGA) test facilities. It was later repainted and put on display at the Aérocampus Aquitaine, an aeronautical and space campus. (Eric Bannwarth)

Chapter 1
The French Navy's Rafale Marines

The origin of Rafale M

While the Mirage 2000 fighter jet was at its final stages of design in the mid-1970s, both the French Air Force and Navy issued their requirements for fourth-generation fighter jets to replace third-generation fighter jets such as the Mirage F1, Jaguar and F-8E. Each had similar requirements for the new fighter jet and to reduce costs, decisions were made to design a common platform, or fighter jet, for them.

The new aircraft was to complement the upcoming and smaller Air Force Dassault Mirage 2000 and the Navy's Super Étendard. However, the new fighter jet was going to be slightly different for each user. Design and development of the new aircraft was delayed for a few years because in 1979 Dassault Aviation Joined West German aerospace manufacturer Messerschmitt-Bölkow-Blohm (MBB) and British Aerospace's (Bae) European Collaborative Fighter (ECF) project, which was later renamed 'European Combat Aircraft' (ECA).

Five years later, France pulled out of the programme and the project for design and development of a new fourth generation fighter jet for the French Air Force and Navy was restarted after the requirements for a carrier-launched fighter jet with a version for land-based operations was reiterated by the French Ministry of Defence. In autumn 1978, just a few months before France joined the ECA, Dassault had already received contracts for the development of Avion de Combat Tactique (ACT 92) (Tactical Combat Aircraft) and despite the fact that the country was part of the international ECA, Dassault continued work on the ACT 92, which later turned into Rafale.

Rafale became an all-weather multi-role fighter jet designed, developed and built in France with the construction of its first demonstrator starting in March 1984 before a contract had been signed with the Directorate General of Armaments (DGA), France's defence procurement agency.

A large delta winged fighter with all-moving canards, equipped with two powerful engines enabling high thrust-to-weight ratio and equipped with a state-of-the-art fly-by-wire system, the first Rafale technology demonstrator was rolled out in December 1985 in Saint-Cloud and logged its maiden flight from Istres-Le Tubé Air Base, the home of Dassault's flight test unit in Southern France on 4 July 1986. The 9.5 tonne (21,000lb) fighter jet climbed to 11km (36,000ft) altitude, reached speed of Mach 1.3 and after the test flight was able to stop after travelling just 300 metres (980ft) on the runway under the control of Dassault's chief test pilot, Guy Mitaux-Maurouard.

The advanced single-seat fighter featured complex swept wings and had composite materials such as carbon fibre and Kevlar, as well as aluminium lithium alloys extensively used during its construction. Originally the Rafale was powered by two General Electric F404-GE-400 turbojet engines with 71.2kN (16,000lb) each. At the end of 1989, the F404 engines were replaced by SNECMA M88-2 turbojet engines.

The Rafale was intended for the Air Force and the Naval Air Force. The Air Force and Naval Air versions became slightly different (larger canard plan, some composite parts were replaced by titanium parts). They were going to replace several military aircraft including the Jaguar, Mirage IVP, Mirage III, Mirage 2000N and D of the Air Force, as well as the Super-Etendard and F-8E Crusader of the Navy. The Rafale Marines were already in service on the Navy's *Charles de Gaulle* within the 12F Flotilla; they also participated in Opération *Heracles* in Afghanistan.

The Rafale's weapon system has evolved over 20 years, with each new evolution becoming known as a standard. Three standards were initially defined (Fl, F2 and F3) and later the F3-R and F4. The F1 standard corresponded to air defence missions (air-to-air missiles), the F2 standard (available in 2005) gave the Rafale ground-attack capabilities, the F3 standard allowed anti-ship warfare, reconnaissance, nuclear strike and in-flight refuelling. In all, the French Defence Ministry ordered 294 aircraft, including 234 for the Air Force (139 two-seaters and 95 single-seaters), and 60 for the Navy (35 two-seaters and 25 single-seaters).

These figures were later reduced to 180 aircraft due to financial reasons and plans for design and development of a two-seater version of Rafale M (Maritime) were cancelled. In total, 48 Rafale Ms were constructed by Dassault including two prototypes, one instructional airframe and 45 serial produced aircraft. They were ordered in four tranches with their deliveries to the French Naval Aviation taking place between 2000 and 2019.

Rafale M uses 80 per cent of the parts of Rafale C (single-seat) and Rafale B (two-seat) operated by the French Air and Space Force. The difference between the Rafale M and Rafale C single-seat is the landing gears. Rafale M uses the Safran Landing System designed for landings and launches from the *Charles de Gaulle* aircraft carrier and all modern-era US Navy aircraft carriers.

The reinforced landing gears enable the aircraft to accelerate quickly from 0 to 240km/h in just three seconds withstanding 90 to 100 tons of pressure. The nose landing gear strut of the aircraft plays a key role in absorbing all of that pressure during the aircraft's catapult launch. The nose gear also has a powerful launch bar, which is lowered and engaged into the catapult launch system of the aircraft carrier for carrier launch. The catapult launches the aircraft with 140 to 170kts, depending on its weight, for 75 metres on the *Charles de Gaulle* aircraft carrier's deck (90 metres on US aircraft carriers).

In addition to the reinforced landing gears, the Rafale M has protective panels beneath the aircraft exhaust nozzles, an arresting hook for landing on the carrier's deck, a Telemir antenna (navigational aid for sea operations) and also a lighting system with three lamps in green, amber and red to guide the pilot during landing on the carrier in order to adjust the angle of attack during the hook landing. The Rafale M has a retractable integrated ladder to facilitate logistical operations on the flight deck.

A starboard bow view of the French *Clemenceau*-class aircraft carrier *Foch* (R-99) as the vessel executes a high-speed turn during exercise Distant Drum on 19 May 1983. This aircraft carrier, similar to its sistership *Clemenceau*, could not host Rafale Ms and as a result both were withdrawn from service and the *Charles de Gaulle* aircraft carrier took their place. (US Department of Defence)

The *Charles de Gaulle* is the most important vessel in the French Navy and a vital asset for Rafale M operations. This image shows the aircraft carrier sailing in the Ionian Sea in March 2022. (Petty Officer 3rd Class Gabriela Chambers / US Navy)

The first production Rafale M with serial number (s/n) 1 is loaded with a buddy inflight refuelling pod under its fuselage during a test flight in the early 2000s. (Katsuhiko Tokunaga / Dassault Aviation)

The first production Rafale M with s/n 1 is loaded with a reconnaissance pod, two external fuel tanks (2,000 litres), four MICA-EM BVRAAMs and two MICA-IR SRAAMs for test purposes on board the *Charles de Gaulle* aircraft carrier on 6 July 2007. (V Almansa / Dassault Aviation)

The first production Rafale M with s/n 1 is loaded with an AM.39 Exocet anti-ship missile for test purposes on 12 March 2005. (V Almansa / Dassault Aviation)

The second Rafale M prototype (M02) during trials on 21 May 2015. It is loaded with a GBU-24 LGB, four MICA-EM BVRAAMs, two MICA-IR SRAAMs, two 2,000-litre external fuel tanks and a Damocles targeting pod. (Photo Sébastien Rande / Dassault Aviation)

Rafale Ms of Flottille 12F: 2001 to today

12F (Flotille or Flotilla) became the first French Navy unit to receive Rafale M fighter jets at Landivisiau Naval Air Station. The unit was a long-time operator of Vought F-8(FN) Crusader fighter jets from 15 October 1964 until the last 12, all upgraded to F-8P standard, were retired from service on 15 December 1999. After an almost 18-month gap, the unit reactivated and received six Rafale Ms from Dassault on 18 May 2001, almost one year after the French Navy received its first two Rafale Ms, serialled 2 and 3, in July 2000.

For almost four decades, the French Navy used Vought F-8 fighter jets for mainly air-to-air missions to complement the fleet of Dassault-Breguet Etendard and Super Etendard, which were used for air-to-ground missions. The Aéronavale initially intended to acquire the McDonnell Douglas F-4B Phantom II for use as an air-superiority fighter jet on its two new aircraft carriers *Clemenceau* and *Foch* but the aircraft was too large and heavy for that purpose. On 16 March 1962, two F-8E fighter jets from the US Navy's VFA-32 flight squadron were flown from the USS *Saratoga* (CV-60) and passed successful carrier trials aboard *Clemenceau*, which led to the French Navy's purchase of 42 of them to equip three Aéronavale's flotillas.

The Vought F-8E (FN)s were delivered between October 1964 and February 1965. For armament, 252 AIM-9E Sidewinder short-range heat-seeking air-to-air missiles were ordered in 1965 and were delivered in 1966 and 1967. The F-8s were modified to carry and use Matra R.530 radar or infrared missiles as an alternative to Sidewinders. The 12F unit, a former operator of Chance Vought F4U-7 Corsair piston-engined fighter jets until 1 August 1963 became their first operator on 15 October 1964.

14F became the second unit after 12F to receive Crusaders from 1 March 1965. Both units had their aircraft upgraded and modified several times during their career including receiving wings of the F-8Js in 1969 and afterburners for their Pratt & Whitney J57-P-20A afterburning turbojet engines. In 1973, they were wired and modified to use R550 Magic IR guided short-range air-to-air missiles and then in 1988, they were modified to use all-aspect R550 Magic-II, while a year later, the ageing Matra 530F missiles were retired leaving Magic-IIs as the sole air-to-air missiles for the French Crusaders. As the programme for the design and development of Dassault Rafale M was delayed, the lifespan of 17 of the surviving F-8Es, all in service with 12F, was extended. These were rewired, their hydraulic systems were refurbished, and their structure was strengthened. They also received new navigation systems and a new radar-warning receiver. These 17 aircraft were named F-8P (P for prolonged). They were often deployed with French Navy carriers during major conflicts and wars but due to the fact that their main role was air-superiority, they were never involved in combat operations directly in the first Gulf War in 1991 and Kosovo in 1999.

Two French Navy Rafales were deployed with the *Charles de Gaulle* aircraft carrier during Mission Héraclès, a French Naval operation in the Afghanistan War against the Taliban and Al-Qaeda in 2001. The aircraft carrier, which had been in construction for almost 14 years, entered service on 18 May 2001. That mission began on 1 December 2001 and the aircraft carrier's involvement ended in April the following year.

The French Task Force, of which the aircraft carrier was a key member, consisted of frigates *La Motte-Picquet*, *Jean de Vienne* and *Jean Bart*, the nuclear attack submarine *Rubis*, the tanker *Meuse* and the *D'Estienne d'Orves-class Corvette* and electronic surveillance vessel *Bougainville*. In addition to the pair of Rafale Ms, 16 Super Étendards, one E-2C Hawkeye airborne early warning and aircraft (AEW&C) and several helicopters were aboard the carrier in the Indian Ocean.

Later, three more Rafale Ms of 12F and one more E-2C joined the aircraft on the carrier. From 19 December, the Super Etendards began reconnaissance and bombing missions (140 missions were performed during the operation); the Rafale Ms stayed behind and performed combat air patrol; at that time they were F1 standard, capable of performing air-superiority missions only. During the operation, Rafale Ms landed on the USS *John C. Stennis* aircraft carrier.

On 25 June 2004, 12F was declared operational three years after it began operating Rafales. Three years later, in 2007, its Rafale Ms participated in the Afghanistan war again and provided close-air-support for the coalition forces. On 28 March 2007, they dropped laser-guided bombs for the first time. The Rafales, which had been deployed with the *Charles de Gaulle* aircraft carrier in the Indian Ocean, had been upgraded to F2 standard. At that time, the 12F had 11 Rafale Ms, which had serial numbers 2 to 12. In 2007, nine more aircraft with serial numbers 13 to 21 were delivered to the squadron.

On 24 September 2009, 12F lost two Rafale Ms with serial numbers 22 and 25. During trials to prepare the Rafale Ms for complete combat readiness prior to their deployment with Task Force 473 in 2010, two French Navy test pilots flew a mission to validate the parameters of catapulting take-off launch under heavy configuration, and the aircraft collided in mid-air. The pilot of one ejected and survived while the other pilot lost his life during the collision.

The French naval task group, designated Task Force 473 and led by *Charles de Gaulle*, departed Toulon on 30 October 2010 for a four-month deployment, code-named Opération *Agapanthus 2010*, to the Mediterranean Sea, Red Sea, Indian Ocean, and Persian Gulf. It was the fourth overseas deployment of the carrier. During that deployment, the Groupe Aéronaval (GAN) had 12 Super Etendard Ms, ten Rafale Ms (from 12F), two E-2Cs and several helicopters on board. One of the Rafale Ms with s/n 18 crashed due to lack of fuel on 28 November 2010. Its pilot ejected and was rescued by a helicopter flown from the GAN while it was operating 97km (60 miles) off the coast of Pakistan in the Arabian Sea in support of coalition forces in Afghanistan.

The French Armed Forces launched Opération *Harmattan* as the French contribution to the 2011 military intervention in Libya in the Libyan Civil War on 19 March that year. Prior to the launch, on 9 March, the French Navy Rafale Ms from 12F on board the *Charles de Gaulle* had performed several reconnaissance missions using Reco NG reconnaissance pods to identify potential targets for the Aéronavale and the French Air Force.

Late on 23 March 2011, several Rafale Ms left the *Charles de Gaulle* aircraft carrier and joined Rafale B/Cs of the FASF. In the early hours of 24 March, they launched multiple SCALP-EG cruise missiles. At the end of the operation on 31 October 2011, 12F's Rafale Ms logged 2,364 flying hours in 616 sorties. They dropped several GBU-12 laser-guided bombs and also launched four SCALP-EG cruise missiles during the entire operation. In addition to the air-to-ground missions, the Rafale Ms equipped with buddy-refuelling pods refuelled the fighter jets participating in long-range operations.

On 19 September 2014, France launched Opération *Chammal in* Iraq and Syria to help contain ISIL. Several months later, on 23 February 2015, the *Charles de Gaulle* carrier strike group arrived at the Persian Gulf with 12 Rafale Ms, nine Super Etendards, one E-2C Hawkeye and four helicopters. The strike participated in the operation for months. The Rafale Ms conducted tens of successful airstrikes, destroying many of their targets.

A French Navy F-8E (FN) Crusader aircraft from 12F lands aboard the nuclear-powered aircraft carrier USS *Dwight D. Eisenhower* **(CVN-69) during flight operations near Toulon, France, on 21 May 1983. (US Department of Defence)**

A French Navy Dassault Rafale M multi-role combat fighter from 12F performs a touch-and-go landing aboard the US Navy (USN) Nimitz Class Aircraft Carrier USS *Dwight D. Eisenhower* (CVN 69), during the multinational maritime exercise (MNME) 05-1 on 25 May 2005. (Phan Peter Carnicelli / US Navy)

Two French Rafale Ms from 12F, two French Super-Etendard Ms and an E-2C Hawkeye from the nuclear-powered aircraft carrier *Charles de Gaulle* (R 91) fly in formation above the flight deck of the Nimitz-class aircraft carrier USS *John C. Stennis* (CVN 74) on 30 May 2005 in the North Arabian Sea. (Mass Communication Specialist Seaman John Wagner / US Navy)

A Rafale M with s/n 19 operated by 12F, approaches for a touch-and-go landing on the flight deck of aircraft carrier USS *Dwight D. Eisenhower* (CVN 69) during a coalition training exercise in the Atlantic Ocean on 19 July 2009. (Mass Communication Specialist 3rd Class Jon Dasbach / US Navy)

A French Rafale M with s/n 38 from 12F receives fuel from an F/A-18E Super Hornet from the Strike Fighter Squadron (VFA) 81 'Sunliners' over the Persian Gulf on 5 March 2015. Two Super Etendard Ms from the French Navy 17F can be seen in the background. (US Navy)

Two Rafale Ms (F2 standard at that time) with s/n 38 and 43 fly over Iraq in support of Operation *Inherent Resolve* on 8 January 2016. (Tech Sgt Nathan Lipscomb / US Air Force)

This Rafale M of Aéronavale with s/n 14 carries four GBU-12 LGBs, two MICA-IR SRAAMs, and two MICA-EM BVRAAMs. Its refuelling probe broke during refuelling over Iraq due to a thunderstorm and tanker pilot error in suddenly reducing speed during Opération *Chammal* on 6 April 2019. (Babak Taghvaee)

In April 2021, Rafale Ms and personnel from 12F participated in the multinational Exercise Iniochos 2021, held and hosted by the Hellenic Air Force at Andravida. The exercise provided an opportunity for Rafale M pilots to practise a series of combined air operations with their Greek and American counterparts. Two Rafale Ms with s/n 11 and 33 are departing the Andravida Air Base on 19 April 2021. (Babak Taghvaee)

A Rafale M from 11F with s/n 11 under the control of a 12F pilot during Exercise Iniochos 2021 on 19 April 2021. It is a common practice for the French Navy flotillas to share their Rafale Ms with each other. (Babak Taghvaee)

An Aéronavale Rafale M with s/n 16 and the insignia of 12F painted on its vertical stabiliser in July 2021. (Babak Taghvaee)

In flight formation are two Rafale Ms with s/n 4 and 27 under the control of 12F pilots with an E-2C airborne early warning and control (AEW&C) aircraft from 4F with s/n 3 and 1666417 US Navy Bureau Number in June 2022. (Babak Taghvaee)

Rafale M with s/n 7 and the insignia of 12F painted on its vertical stabiliser in July 2022. (Babak Taghvaee)

From front to back are 26, 6 and 12; three Rafale Ms from 12F in September 2022. (Babak Taghvaee)

This Rafale M with s/n 6 is armed with two MICA-IR SRAAMs and two MICA-EM BVRAAMs while in use by 12F in September 2022. (Babak Taghvaee)

Rafale Ms of Flottille 11F: 2011 to today

Between 2007 and 2016, Aéronavale received 25 more Rafale Ms enabling it to equip two more squadrons with the aircraft type as a replacement for their ageing Super Etendards at Landivisiau Naval Air Base. 11F was the first and had operated the Super Etendard from September 1978. Prior to that aircraft, the squadron had operated Etendard IVM from 1 April 1963.

11Fs transition to Rafale Ms began on 19 September 2011. The unit received six Rafale Ms in that year. One of them, with s/n 24, was lost during a simulated dogfight against an F/A-18E Super Hornet from the US Navy flown from the USS *Eisenhower* aircraft carrier in the Mediterranean.

Gradually, the Super Etendard Ms were retired or transferred to 17F, which remained the last operator of the aircraft type until 2016. During 2011–16, 15 Super Etendard M pilots transitioned to Rafale Ms by September 2016. This was later increased to 19 pilots in 2020.

Starting from 1 October 2016, the *Charles de Gaulle* carrier strike group took part in Opération *Chammal*, this time with only Rafale M fighter jets, which were from 11F and 12F. It was the third time that the *Charles de Gaulle* aircraft carrier had participated in the operation but the first time for the Rafale Ms. In total 23 Rafale Ms with s/n 8, 9, 10, 13, 14, 15, 19, 21, 26, 28, 30, 31, 32, 35, 36, 38, 39, 41, 42, 43, 44, 45 and 46 took part. In addition, two E-2Cs with s/n 2 and 3 from 4F; an SE.3160 Alouette III with s/n 219 from 22 Squadron; two SA.365F1s with s/n 313 and 318 from 35F; and an NH90 NFH with s/n 8 from 33F took part.

On 1 October, the GAN carried out its first combat missions against ISIL from the eastern Mediterranean while it was located in south Cyprus. The first airstrikes hit an ISIL fighting position in northwest Ramadi, central Iraq, while two E-2C Hawkeyes were performing surveillance. On the same day, a French Navy Atlantique 2 Maritime Patrol Aircraft with s/n 23 from Jordan, and a GAN Rafale M carried out three intelligence/surveillance/reconnaisance (ISR) sorties over Iraq and Syria. To support the GAN operations, the French Navy had forward-deployed a second ATL2 of 21F squadron with s/n 28 to Paphos International Airport in Cyprus while the first ATL2 with s/n 23 had been deployed to Muwaffaq al-Salti AB in Jordan on 10 February 2016.

Between 1 and 6 October, a total of 63 combat sorties were carried out by the French Navy's Rafale Ms and ATL2s and the French Air Force's Rafale Cs from Air Base (BA) 104 at Al-Dhafra. They consisted of ISR sorties of Rafale M and ATL2s; and 50 armed / combat reconnaissance and pre-planned close air support (CAS) sorties by the Rafale Ms which resulted in 15 airstrikes. In the next few days, seven more ISR sorties were carried out by the French Navy Rafale Ms and ATL2s, while two E-2Cs from the *Charles de Gaulle* carried out five airborne command and control and electronic warfare (EW) missions. At the same time, 44 combat reconnaissance, strike and pre-planned sorties were carried out by the French Navy's Rafale Ms. Between 17 and 20 October, nine ISR sorties were performed by the French Navy ATL2s and French Air Force's Rafale Cs.

One of the most important airstrikes took place on 15 and 16 October 2016. During the airstrike three French Air Force Rafale Cs together with four Navy Rafale Ms launched eight general purpose long-range stand-off cruise missiles (SCALP EG) at an improvised explosive device (IED) factory which was 30km (18 miles) south of Mosul while simultaneously an E-2C monitored air-space over the operation.

Between 17 and 21 October, the *Charles de Gaulle*'s carrier operations stopped after it went to the Port of Limassol, Cyprus, for resupply and replenishment. Soon after returning to its position south of Cyprus, its Rafale Ms together with the French Air Force's Rafale Cs logged 68 armed reconnaissance sorties during which 64 targets were destroyed in 49 airstrikes between 21 and 28 October. In the same period, nine ISR missions were carried out by the two ATL2s, as well as Rafale Ms.

On 31 October, during an air raid performed by 20 fighter aircraft from seven members of OIR-CJTF (Operation *Inherent Resolve* – Combined Joint Task Force), two French Navy Rafale Ms accompanied by four French Air Force Rafale Cs carried out an airstrike against a weapons' manufacturing and storage complex in Haditha, Iraq. That night, eight SCALP-EGs were launched at the target by the Rafales. Before the operation, one of the French Navy's ATL2s had performed an ISR sortie over the target, then after the airstrike, aircrew of another ATL2 carried out a battle damage assessment (BDA) mission.

The Iraqi security forces' operation to enter the city of Mosul began on 1 November using artillery barrage, tank and machine gun fire all focussed on ISIL positions. Subsequently, all coalition air forces including the United States Air Force (USAF) during Opération *Inherent Resolve*, the RAF during Opération *Shader* (a Tornado GR.4 with ZA601 tail code), and the French Air Force and Navy during Opération *Chammal*, provided close air support for the ground forces entering the city.

Between 28 October and 2 November 2016, 98 combat sorties were logged by the French Air Force and French Navy during Opération *Chammal* during which 17 airstrikes including 13 close air support sorties were performed in support of Iraqi forces trying to enter Mosul on 1 and 2 November 2016. Between 5 and 10 November, the Iraqi Popular Mobilization Forces and Kurdish Peshmerga reached

Tel-Afar and liberated Bashiqa town respectively. In this period, the French Air Force and Navy provided air support for them as well as for the Iraqi Special Forces and Army, which were fighting ISIL in the main axis in Mosul. In total, 70 combat sorties were performed consisting of nine ISR sorties by ATL2s and Rafale Ms, five airborne command and control sorties by the E-2Cs, and 56 armed reconnaissance sorties by the Rafale Ms and Rafale Cs during which 11 targets were detected and destroyed in ten airstrikes.

Fifty combat sorties were carried out by French combat aircraft between 21 and 24 November including, six ISR sorties carried out by ATL2s and Rafale Ms, one sortie carried out by an E-2C, and 44 armed reconnaissance sorties carried out by Rafale Cs and Rafale Ms. In total, 14 targets were destroyed with 13 airstrikes including seven in Mosul and three in the north of Raqqa, Syria. This was in support of Kurdish forces, which had started an offensive against ISIL earlier in that region to draw ISIL to its Syrian fronts in order to reduce pressure on Mosul.

Between 24 November and 1 December 2016, during Opération *Chammal*, 97 combat sorties were carried out by French combat aircraft consisting of five ISR sorties, seven airborne command-and-control sorties by two E-2Cs from the aircraft carrier, and 85 armed reconnaissance sorties resulting in the destruction of 24 targets in 14 airstrikes (11 in Iraq and three in Syria).

On 29 November 2016, four French Air Force Rafale Cs and two French Navy Rafale Ms successfully launched eight SCALP-EG cruise missiles against several Daesh facilities southwest of Raqqa. This strike destroyed a chemical weapon laboratory or factory and a weapons storage facility. The mission

A Dassault Super Étendard with s/n 54 (c/n 60) from 11F, and an F-8E(FN) Crusader with s/n 19 (c/n 1236) parked on the flight deck of the *Clemenceau* (R 98) on 7 November 1988. (US Department of Defence)

was commanded and supervised by the OIR-CJTF's HQ in Kuwait while the Combined Air Operations Center (CAOC), headquartered at Al-Udeid, Qatar, performed this operation.

By the end of November, less than 30 per cent of the area of Mosul east of the Tigris had been liberated, and the Iraqi armed forces had taken control of 19 neighbourhoods in eastern Mosul during the month. On 30 November, the people's mobilisation force (PMF) announced that they had liberated 12 villages from ISIL/Daesh in the Tal Afar area over the previous five days.

During the French Navy sea operations, the sole SE.3160 Alouette III hovered beside the *Charles de Gaulle* carrier to quickly provide medical evacuation (MEDEVAC) and search and rescue (SAR) for pilots of any Rafale M who had crashed in daylight, while two Dauphins did the same job but at night.

Like many of the aircraft carriers, the *Charles de Gaulle* has its own fleet of airborne early warning and control aircraft consisting of two E-2Cs of the French Naval Aviation's 4F squadron, which has three of these aircraft in its service. They are always airborne even when a single Rafale M is performing a combat mission in order to monitor airspace around it and protect it from the danger of unwanted confrontation. Each flight sortie of an E-2C lasted almost ten hours.

Deployment of the French Navy Carrier Battle Group to the Mediterranean Sea ended on 15 December 2016 and the carrier headed back to France. However, French Naval Aviation continued its presence in Opération *Chammal* by means of an ATL2 based in Jordan, which can be used in ISR and BDA missions or armed-reconnaissance missions because of its ability to carry and use four GBU-12 Paveway II LGBs in its bomb bay for precision bombings.

A year after later, the French Navy deployed several Rafale Ms from 11F and 12F to Prince Hassan Air Base (H4) in Jordan from where they conducted several combat missions in Iraq and Syria as part of Opération *Chammal*.

Several Rafale Ms from Aéronavale including s/n 14, 26, 44 and 46 from 11F during deployment to the eastern Mediterranean in November 2016. They can be seen on the deck of the carrier during its port visit from Limassol on 17 November 2016. (Babak Taghvaee)

The *Charles de Gaulle* aircraft carrier carrying Rafale Ms from 11F and 12F during its deployment to the Mediterranean for participation in the Opération *Chammal*; it can be seen exiting the port of Limassol on 21 November 2016. (Babak Taghvaee)

A Rafale M, with s/n 35 equipped with an inflight refuelling pod, can be seen refuelling another with s/n 6. They were under the control of 11F pilots. (Babak Taghvaee)

Two of Aéronavale's Rafale Ms are flying in formation while under the control of pilots from 11F in June 2022. (Babak Taghvaee)

Rafale M with s/n 27 under the control of an 11F pilot in June 2022. (Babak Taghvaee)

A French Navy Rafale M with s/n 28 performs a touch-and-go landing on the flight deck of the aircraft carrier USS *Dwight D. Eisenhower* (CVN 69) on 8 December 2016. (Petty Officer 3rd Class Christopher A Michaels / US Navy)

This image, taken in the Mediterranean Sea on 8 December 2016, shows a French Navy Rafale M with s/n 19 in the use of 11F from the aircraft carrier FS *Charles de Gaulle*. It is performing a touch-and-go-landing on the flight deck of USS *Dwight D. Eisenhower* (CVN 69). (Petty Officer 3rd Class Christopher A Michaels / US Navy)

Rafale Ms of Flottille 17F: 2016 to today

From September 2011, the Flotilla 17F, nicknamed 'La glorieuse', had become the final operator of Super Etendard M fighter jets and now with a total of 41 Rafale Ms in service, including four in use for pilot training at Saint-Dizier Robinson Air Base, the French Navy could finally equip its last unit. In July 2016, 17F became the third flotilla of the Aéronavale to be equipped with Rafale M multi-role fighter jets.

The *Charles de Gaulle* aircraft carrier had its mid-life major technical rework (ATM) beginning in 2017 for several months, which deprived 17F pilots of the opportunity to practise deck landing and launch for months. In that period, 12F's Rafale Ms were involved in Opération *Chammal* and some were deployed to Prince Hassan Air Base in the Royal Jordanian Air Force. In 2018, 17F became fully operational and ready for combat and as a result, its pilots, ground crew and Rafale Ms were deployed to the Mediterranean and later Persian Gulf to take part in Opération *Chammal*.

At the start of February 2022, 17F was one of two French Navy units to be deployed with *Charles de Gaulle* to join USS *Harry S. Truman* aircraft carrier and form Carrier Strike Group 8. Operations were co-ordinated in the Mediterranean Sea. The aircraft carriers contributed to the defence of the Eastern flank of NATO as well as controlling the airspace over the Mediterranean Sea. In the air, their Rafale Ms and F/A-18E/F multi-role fighter jets participated in NATO's enhanced Vigilance Activities (eVA) in Romanian and Bulgarian airspace.

From 9 February to 3 March 2022, Rafale Ms from GAN carried out their seventh series of airstrikes against ISIL/Daesh since the start of Opération *Chammal*, conducting more than 70 operational sorties in more than 400 hours in support of the Iraqi armed forces.

On 24 February 2022, Russian armed forces invaded Ukraine and in response NATO increased its air-policing missions over its eastern flanks. Rafale Ms from 17F on board the *Charles de Gaulle* began combat air patrols over the Black Sea and Romania, with air-refuelling support provided by the Airbus A330-243MRTT Phoenix, C-135FR and KC-135RG tanker aircraft of the French Air and Space Force. During those missions, Rafale Ms were flying from the aircraft carrier, which was positioned in Greek territorial waters in the Aegean Sea.

During most of the combat air patrol (CAP) missions, the Rafale Ms carried a pair of MICA-EM active radar homing medium-range air-to-air missiles and a pair of MICA-IR infrared guided short-range air-to-air missiles. In several cases, they also had two Meteor missiles, the next generation of beyond visual range air-to-air missile (BVRAAM). During these missions, an E-2C of the Aéronavale supported the Rafale Ms on CAP duty.

On 7 April 2022, the *Charles de Gaulle* returned to the port of Toulon from the Clemenceau-22 deployment mission while its fighter jets including Rafale Ms from 17F, flew to Landivisiau, France, a few days earlier. It was not long before the carrier returned to the sea and the Rafale Ms from 17F joined it on 30 April 2022.

On 1 May, the aircraft carrier and fighter jets were used by several Rafale pilots to regain their carrier operations' qualifications for incoming deployments. In June 2022, some of these pilots and their Rafale Ms participated in an exercise named Ocean Hit 2022. The exercise involved 30 Rafale Ms, an E-2C AEW&C aircraft, an NH90-NFH Caiman helicopter and an Atlantic 2 maritime patrol aircraft from Aéronavale, while the FASF participated with its Mirage 2000D, Mirage 2000-5F and Rafale B/C fighter jets and an E-3CF Sentry AWACS aircraft. The Swiss Air Force also joined with its F/A-18A/B Legacy Hornets, the Hellenic Air Force with its F-16C/D Block 30s, and the Royal Air Force with its F-35B Lightning IIs.

French Navy Rafale Ms today

The French Navy currently has 41 Rafale Ms of which 37 are in service with three flotillas in Landivisiau while four are in service with Escadron de Transformation Rafale (ETR) 3/4 'Aquitaine' of the FASF in BA113 Saint-Dizier. The latter four aircraft are used for the French Navy Rafale fighter pilot-training programme.

Rafale M pilots must first pass basic flight training on SR20 and SR22 ultralight aircraft at Salon de Provence. They move on to fly with Grob G120A-F light training aircraft at the FASF's EIV 2/12 at Picardie at Cognac. Finally, they progress to PC-21 advanced training aircraft at the same base. After graduation from the undergraduate pilot-training course, pilots are sent to the US where they train on the US Navy's McDonnell Douglas T-45C Goshawk advanced jet trainers, including carrier launch and landings. As pilots pass through the T-45 pilot-training course and graduate successfully, they return to France and move on to the Rafale pilot-training course at ETR 3/4 Aquitaine. Initially they fly with Rafale Bs and after several training sorties, fly a solo flight on a Rafale M. Pilots progress to join one of three flotillas operating the Rafale Ms until they reach complete operational and combat readiness for overseas deployments with the GAN.

Rafale Ms of the Aéronavale were upgraded seven times by February 2023. Upgrades included the capability to use MICA air-to-air missiles and SCALP EG cruise missiles after upgrade to F2 standard, the capability to use AM.39 Exocet anti-ship missiles after upgrade to F3 standard, the capability to use GB-24 laser-guided bombs as a result of an upgrade to F3.3 standard, and finally the capability to use the SBU-54 LGB, GBU-16 LGB, Talios new generation laser designation pod (PDL NG), the new Reco NG reconnaissance pod and the new Meteor air-to-air missile as a result of upgrade to F3-R standard between 2018 and 2020.

These Super Etendard Ms from 17F flew above the aircraft carrier USS *Harry S. Truman* (CVN 75), which was assigned to French Task Force 473 on 1 January 2014. Two years later, the flotilla replaced these with Rafale Ms. (Communication Specialist 3rd Class Karl Anderson / US Navy)

The French Navy's Rafale Marines

S/n 2 is currently the oldest Rafale M serving in the French Navy. When it was pictured here it was in use by 17F. It is landing on USS *George H.W. Bush* (CVN 77) aircraft carrier on 10 May 2018. (Mass Communication Specialist 3rd Class Zachary P Wickline / US Navy)

A French Rafale M F-3R standard assigned to 17F landing on the flight deck of USS *Harry S. Truman* (CVN 75). Despite having insignia from 12F on its tail, the aircraft was under control of a 17F pilot on 11 March 2022. (Mass Communication Specialist 3rd Class Tate Cardinal / US Navy)

Every year during the Bastille Day Parade on 14 July, seven Rafale Ms, accompanied by an E-2C Hawkeye-2000 from 4F fly over Paris. In 2022, a 17F pilot led one of the Rafale M formations. (Babak Taghvaee)

On 9 September 2021, two Rafale Ms with s/n 36 and 41 flew in formation with two F4U Corsair World War Two-era fighters during the Air Legend airshow South of Paris on 12 September 2021. (Babak Taghvaee)

The French Navy's Rafale Marines

Two French Navy Rafale Ms operated by 17F during an interoperability exercise in the US Central Command area of responsibility on 12 December 2022. (SSgt Gerald R Willis / US Air Force)

Two Rafale Ms with s/n 36 and 41 have extended arrester hooks while flying in formation with the ignited afterburners of their Snecma M88-2 Turbofan engines. They were under control of 17F pilots. (Babak Taghvaee)

A French Navy Rafale M with s/n 16 operated by 17F before receiving fuel from a USAF KC-135R while over Iraq during Opération *Chammal*. It can be seen armed with two French-made SBU-54 LGBs on 14 April 2021. (Senior Airman Brandon Cribelar / US Air Force)

Chapter 2
Rafale B/Cs of the French Air and Space Force

Rafale B/Cs from ECE 1/30 Côte d'Argent: 2003 to today

In February 2023, the French Air and Space Force (FASF) operated 95 Rafale B/C multi-role fighter jets. Among these, one Rafale B and a Rafale C were in use with the flight unit (EV) of the Directorate General of Armament (DGA) at Istres-Le Tubé Air Base (Base aérienne 125 Istres le tubé) while two Rafale Bs were in use with Dassault Aviation's flight test unit at the same air base.

In addition to these four aircraft for test purposes, four other aircraft comprising a Rafale C and three Rafale Bs are in similar use by the French Air and Space Force at the Fighter and Experimentation Squadron (ECE) 1/30 'Côte d'Argent' at Air Base 118 Mont-de-Marsan. This leaves 87 Rafale B/Cs in use with four fighter, and one training, squadron at two air bases.

On 1 July 1965, the Centre d'expertise aérienne militaire or CEAM (Military Air Expertise Centre) officially created Fighter Squadron (EC) 5/330 'Cote d'Argent', which for 30 years tested various combat aircraft and their weapons including Mirage III, Jaguar, Mirage F1, Alphajet and Mirage 2000.

The French Air Force received its first Rafale C with s/n 101 on 16 April 2003. The aircraft was handed over for flight testing and, after a few months, was delivered to EC 5/330 alongside three Rafale Bs with s/n 301, 302 and 303. They were used to prepare the first pilots from EC 1/7 Provence, which began operating Rafale Cs from June 2005 and Rafale Bs from June 2006.

In 2007, the EC 5/330 was reorganised as ECE (Fighter and Experimentation Squadron) 5/330. After the recreation of the 30th Fighter Wing at BA118 Mont-de-Marsan in 2015, it became ECE 1/30 from 1 March 2016. The EC 1/30 has two Escadrilles (small units), which are BR127 Le Tigre and BR128 Le Scarabée Blanc. Each Escadrille has a group of fighter jets and several air and ground crews.

Since the beginning of the squadron's Rafale operations, its aircraft, alongside its test pilots and navigators, have often participated in overseas operations. For example, in March 2011, the squadron had one of its Rafale Bs with s/n 305 and 118-EC code assigned to the EC 1/7, which had seven Rafale B/Cs on deployment at BA126 Solenzara. The Rafale B alongside Rafale B/Cs of EC 1/7 flew combat missions during Opération *Harmattan* in Libya. In addition, the ECE 1/30's Mirage 2000Ds were involved in Opération *Barkhane* against Al-Qaeda-affiliated terrorist groups in Africa.

On 20 and 21 June 2021, two Rafale Cs (one from RC 2/30 Normandie-Niemen and one from ETR 3/4 Aquitaine) and a Rafale B (from ECE 1/30) supported by two Airbus A330-243 MRTT Phoenix tanker aircraft and two Airbus A400M Atlas heavy transport aircraft, flew to French Polynesia in less than 40 hours after leaving Istres, Mont-de-Marsan and Saint-Dizier during a Mission named 'Haifara Waeka'. The aircraft flew over Iceland, Greenland and Canada before landing on the American air base of Travis in California on 20 June.

After 12 hours' rest, they resumed their mission over the Pacific Ocean towards Papeete. The mission was a simulation of an airstrike by the French Air Force's Air Planning and Operations Centre (CAPCO) to protect the French overseas territories in the shortest possible time. This mission involved a Rafale B with s/n 309 and 30 HB code and two aircrew from ECE 1/30. On their way back to France, the Rafales participated in a joint exercise with F-22A Raptor air-superiority fighter jets from the Hawaii Air National Guard, USAF, based at Joint Base Pearl Harbor-Hickam from 27 June to 5 July 2021.

Today, ECE 1/30 conducts more than 70 experiments on airborne weapon systems and their associated systems as well as the evaluation of simulation and decision support software. It ensures the transformation of flight personnel, mechanics, electronic warfare specialists and simulator instructors on new equipment in service with the Air Force. The squadron will soon evaluate and test the Rafale C/Bs of the FASF which have been built or upgraded to F4 standard.

Today, EC 1/30 is still operating a Mirage 2000D with s/n 637 and 30-XQ code, and it has three Rafale Bs, which are 304/30-EB, 309/30-HB and 329/30-ID in addition to a Rafale C, which is 113/30-IP. In 2021 and 2022, the squadron tested and evaluated three Mirage 2000D RMVs, which had recently been upgraded for the FASF. Its sole Mirage 2000D with s/n 637 is also upgraded to the RMV standard.

Right: Two Rafale Bs with s/n 301 and 302 and the second Rafale M prototype (M02) at Dassault Aviation's facility in Istres on 7 November 2010. (V Almansa / Dassault Aviation)

Below: First production Rafale B with s/n 301 receives fuel from the first production Rafale M with s/n 1 during a test flight in 2003. The 301 was operated by the ECE 1/30 for several years before being returned to the Dassault test centre in Istres. (Katsuhiko Tokunaga)

309/30-HB, one of three Rafale Bs from ECE 1/30 participated in a joint exercise with the Hawaii Air National Guard on 30 June 2021 when it was pictured with this US ANG's F-22A over the Pacific Ocean. (SSgt Orlando Corpuz / US Air Force)

309/30-HB is one of three Rafale Bs operated by ECE 1/30 for test purposes. It received this special paint scheme before participating in NATO Tiger Meet 2022 at Araxos Air Base in 2022. (Babak Taghvaee)

329/30-ID, one of three Rafale Bs from ECE 1/30 during the exercise Atlantic Trident-2021 at BA118 Mont-de-Marsan on 25 May 2021. (Babak Taghvaee)

The sole Rafale C of ECE 1/30 equipped with a Damocles multifunction pod during the exercise Atlantic Trident-2021 at BA118 Mont-de-Marsan on 25 May 2021. (Babak Taghvaee)

Rafale B/Cs of EC 1/7 Provence: 2005 to today

EC 1/7 'Provence' an operator of SEPECAT Jaguar ground-attack aircraft at BA113 Saint-Dizier until 2005, became the first fighter squadron to operate Dassault Rafale B/C multi-role fighter jets in the French Air and Space Force. While the first production Rafale C, with construction number (c/n) 101, was delivered to ECE 1/30, the second production Rafale C with c/n 102 was delivered to EC 1/7 Provence in June 2005.

Almost a year later, the squadron received its first Rafale B with s/n 304 on 26 June 2006. Rafale B was a two-seater aircraft with the secondary role of transition-training Rafale pilots. There were no other differences in its mission capabilities compared to Rafale C.

It wasn't long before EC 1/7 gained its initial combat readiness in 2007. In January of that year, the squadron had 20 Rafale B/Cs. On 12 March 2007, three of them, all Rafale B variants with s/n 312, 314 and 318 at F2 standard at that time, were deployed to Dushanbe, Tajikistan's province to take part in the war against the Taliban during Operation *Enduring Freedom*.

Just two days after their arrival, the aircraft, each armed with four GBU-12 LGBs, began armed patrols over Afghanistan. At the same time, Rafale Ms, also F2 standard, from 12F Flotilla, on deployment with the *Charles de Gaulle* in the North Arabian Sea, began their operational involvement in the war in Afghanistan. The first GBU-12 was dropped by a Navy Rafale M on 28 March, and later an Air Force Rafale B dropped its first GBU-12s in Helmand province on 1 April 2007.

The initial deployment of the Rafale Bs from EC 1/7 lasted for three months until June 2007. The squadron's Rafales were again deployed to the Afghanistan war from March to June 2008. This time, in addition to GBU-12s, they also carried Armement Air-Sol Modulaire (AASM or HAMMER), a French precision-guided munition developed by Safran Electronics & Defense. On 19 April 2008, the first was deployed.

EC 1/7 also took part in Opération *Harmattan* against Libyan Armed Forces in 2011. While Rafale Ms from 12F participated in Opération *Harmattan* from its home aircraft carrier on 22 March 2011, eight Rafales from EC 1/7 from BA113, mainly single seaters (Rafale C), participated in the war directly from BA113 thanks to the C-135FR tanker aircraft and E-3CF AEW&C from 19 March 2011. Each one of them had two MICA-IR SRAAMs and four MICA-EM BVRAAMs. They also have three external fuel tanks.

For the reconnaissance missions, the Rafale Cs carried and successfully tested the Reco NG reconnaissance pods for the first time, while for the strike missions, each Rafale B or C carried four AASMs. The first two Rafale Cs that performed combat air patrol (CAP) over Libya carrying MICA IR/EM missiles had s/n 110/30-IN and 112/30-IQ. Later, five Rafale B/Cs from EC 1/7 and EC 1/4 were deployed to Naval Air Station (NAS) Sigonella, in Italy, from where they conducted armed patrols over Libya.

To shorten the flight from France to Libya and increase the duration of each armed patrol mission, particularly for the Rafales armed with AASM bombs, eight other Rafale B/Cs were forward deployed to BA126 Solenzara, which is situated 830km (515 miles) closer to Libya. Some of the first examples to participate in those missions were a Rafale C, 113/113-IR, and two Rafale Bs known as 305/118-EC and 333/113-IH. They each carried four AASMs, two MICA-EMs and two MICA-IRs in addition to three external fuel tanks. Among these, 305/118-EC was not originally from EC 1/7 but had been borrowed from ECE 1/30 and was being flown by its test pilot and navigator. For the first time, these Rafale B/Cs used Damocles targeting pods for dropping their AASMs.

During Opération *Harmattan*, 13 Rafale B/Cs from the French Air Force, mainly from EC 1/7, carried out 4,569 hours of combat flights in 1,039 sorties. They dropped 288 GBU-12 LGBs, 155 DBU-22 training bombs (training variant of GBU-22), 77 GBU-49 LGBs, 44 GBU-24 LGBs and 139 AASM LGBs. They also launched 11 SCALP-EG cruise missiles.

Since 24 June 2016, EC 1/7 Provence has been on deployment at BA104 at Al-Dhafra Air Base, United Arab Emirates. Before that, the squadron's Rafales were directly involved in two other wars.

From January 2013, the Rafales participated in Opération *Serval* in Mali and later, from December 2013, in Opération *Sangaris* in the Central African Republic. Also during Opération *Chammal*, its Rafales were often deployed to Prince Hassan Air Base (H-4) in Jordan from where they conducted airstrikes in Iraq from 2014, and then in Syria from 2015.

On 6 December 2007, EC 1/7 lost a Rafale B with s/n 316 and 7-HL code. The aircraft and pilot were lost due to the pilot's spatial disorientation during a training flight near Neuvic, Corrèze.

As of February 2023, five Rafale Cs were in use by EC 1/7 at Abu-Dhabi; they originally belonged to the 30th Combat Wing of the French Air and Space Force in BA118 Mont-de-Marsan. They are 130/7-GI, 132/7-GK, 137/7-GP, 138/7-GQ and 148/7-VA. In addition, a sixth aircraft with s/n 107 and 113-HJ code stored in Mont-de-Marsan is believed to be the property of EC 1/7. Among the five airworthy Rafale Cs of EC 1/7 in Abu-Dhabi, the aircraft with s/n 137 is earmarked for delivery to Greece in 2023 or 2024.

Rafale C with s/n 137 became the first equipped with RBE-2 AESA radar in September 2012. The aircraft was delivered to the military air expertise centre (CEAM) in September 2012, was tested by DGA-EV in October of that year and finally transferred to EC 1/7 'Provence'. All of the Rafale B/Cs produced to F3-04T standard by Dassault between 2012 and 2018 had Active Electronically Scanned Array (AESA) radars. All Rafales manufactured before 2012 were later equipped with the radar during their modernisation to the F3-ORT and F3-R standards.

A French Air Force Jaguar A/E fighter-bomber aircraft flies a refuelling mission over the Adriatic Sea, in support of Operation *Joint Forge* on 7 April 2004. This aircraft was one of the last Jaguar fighter jets to serve with the EC 1/7 Provence before the squadron's conversion to Rafales a few years after this image was taken. (Tech Sgt Mike Buytas / US Air Force)

Left: Rafale C137 was the first European combat aircraft equipped with an active phased array radar (RBE2 AESA). Istres, 11 December 2008. (Eric Raz / Thales)

Below: A French Rafale B fighter aircraft from EC 1/7 Provence armed with four GBU-12 LGBs. It is seen before refuelling from a KC-135R Stratotanker from the USAF on 23 April 2013 during Opération *Serval* over Mali. (1st Lt Christopher Mesnard / US Air Force)

Two French Rafale fighter aircraft from EC 1/7 Provence are each armed with four GBU-12 LGBs and are about to refuel from a USAF KC-135R Stratotanker on 23 April 2013. The Stratotankers from the 100th Air Refuelling Wing at RAF Mildenhall supported Rafales from EC 1/7 during Opération *Serval*. (1st Lt Christopher Mesnard / US Air Force)

A Rafale C from EC 1/7 Provence is armed with four SBU-54 AASMs, two MICA-IR SRAAMs (on the wing tip launchers) and two MICA-EMs BVRAAMs (not visible) and is receiving fuel from a USAF KC-135R tanker over Iraq during Opération *Chammal* on 31 August 2017. (SSgt Trevor McBride / US Air Force)

A French Air Force Rafale refuels from a KC-135 Stratotanker from the 340th Expeditionary Air Refuelling Squadron over Iraq in support of Operation *Inherent Resolve* on 1 November 2017. The Rafale is capable of supporting the full mission spectrum: air superiority, fighter escort, reconnaissance, aerial refuelling, close air support, air defence suppression and precision strikes. (US Air Force photo by Tech Sgt Gregory Brook)

Rafale Bs of EC 1/4 Gascogne: 2008 to today

The 4th Combat Wing of the FASF at BA113 Saint-Dizier operated 47 Rafale Bs as of February 2023. Among these, nine were in service with ETR 3/4 Aquitaine for Rafale pilot training, while the rest were shared by the escadrilles (small aircraft units operating one to six aircraft) of two fighter squadrons, the EC 1/4 Gascogne and EC 2/4 La Fayette. Both squadron's primary role is nuclear deterrence by means of air-sol moyenne portée-A (ASMP-A) nuclear air-launched cruise missiles. Both of these fighter squadrons are key units of the French Strategic Air Forces, a subordinate of the FASF.

The Gascogne squadron was originally created as Bomber Group 2/19 equipped with Bloch MB.210 twin-engined heavy bombers on 1 April 1937. Its escadrilles were two World War One veterans, SAL28 'Elephant' and SPA79 'Wolf'. Gascogne was later redesignated as Bomber Group 1/19 on 1 September 1940. On 21 February 1944, the unit was reorganised as Medium Bomber Group 1/19 Gascogne. From September 1945 until it was dissolved in April 1946 it was based at Mengen.

In 1940, one of the Bomber Group's escadrilles received Douglas DB-7 bombers (a French version of the US Douglas A-20 Havoc) and used them against German forces during the Battle of France but after several losses their surviving examples were taken to Africa. After the liberation of France, the surviving DB-7s were flown to mainland France between late 1944 and early 1945 and were used alongside Martin B-26 Marauders from the Gascogne Bomber Group against isolated German forces on the western coast.

The Bomber Group was officially reconstructed at Tourane as Bomber Squadron in January 1951 in order to take part in the Indochina War. After that war, it was repatriated to Bordeaux and it was again disbanded on 17 September 1962. The unit operated A-26B and B-26C Invaders at this time.

Two years later, on 1 June 1964, Bomber Squadron 1/91 Gascogne was reformed in Mont-de-Marsan and turned into the first nuclear-capable squadron with its Mirage IV bombers, which were declared operational on 1 October 1964. On 19 July 1966, a Mirage IV from the squadron dropped an AN-22 nuclear bomb in the Pacific Experimentation Centre. Earlier, on 10 May that year, a Mirage IVA with s/n 36 had logged its first transatlantic flight by means of three inflight refuellings to reach Boston in 7 hours and 40 minutes.

Bomber Squadron (EB) 1/91 trained its crew for low-altitude bombardment in 1968. The squadron received Mirage IVPs and from 1986, had eight of them modified to use ASMP nuclear cruise missiles. Six years later, in 1992, the squadron also received CT-52 reconnaissance pods for use on its Mirage IVPs for tactical reconnaissance. Such missions were performed in support of a peace-keeping mission in Bosnia-Herzegovina.

In 1996, after the Air Force's Mirage 2000Ns became fully operational, EB 1/91 changed status and became a Strategic Reconnaissance Squadron with its CT-52 pods and their OMERA cameras. Reconnaissance missions were performed by the squadron over Hanish Islands in the Red Sea during Opération *Condor* (flown from Djibouti) in 1996 and 1997, Opération *Aladdin* in Iraq in 1998, Opération *Heracles* in Afghanistan in 2001 and 2002, and finally Opération *Tarpan* in Iraq in 2003. Two years later, on 23 June 2005, the Distant Strategic Squadron 1/91 was disbanded at Mont-de-Marsan and a Mirage IVP from that squadron with s/n 59 logged its last flight under the control of the squadron's chief of operations, Eric Pintat.

On 1 September 2008, Gascogne was reformed as Fighter Squadron (EC) 1/91 at BA113 after it received its first Rafale B (F3 standard). The squadron's primary purpose was now nuclear deterrence and its secondary task was conventional strike. For that purpose, its Rafale Bs were equipped with weapon systems to carry and use ASMP missiles. In July 2010, the squadron carried out its first nuclear alert from BA113 Saint-Dizier.

In 2011, the EC 1/91 participated in the Opération *Harmattan* against Libyan Armed Forces still loyal to Colonel Gaddafi. The squadron's Rafale Bs initially participated in combat air patrols and reconnaissance missions directly from BA113 but later some were deployed to NAS Sigonella in Italy from where they carried out 368 sorties over Libya and dropped 120 bombs, mainly AASMs.

In 2013, EC 1/91 had personnel and aircraft involved in Opération *Serval* against Ansar Dine and Movement for Unity and Jihad in West Africa (MUJAO) and Al-Qaeda in the Islamic Maghreb (AQIM) in Mali. On 14 January 2013, the French Air Force deployed two Rafale Bs and four Rafale Cs from EC 1/91, EC 1/7 and RC 2/30 to N'Djamena to take part in the operation. The Rafale Bs were from Gascogne squadron. The next day, two Mirage F1CR tactical reconnaissance aircraft from Reconnaissance Squadron 2/33 Savoie were also deployed to N'Djamena to support the Rafale operations. These Rafales dropped tens of GBU-12s and AASM LGBs during the operation, which lasted until July 2014.

During Opération *Chammal*, which initially had French Navy Rafales and French Air Force Rafale B/Cs from Lorraine squadron (based at Abu-Dhabi) involved, the Rafale Bs of EC 1/91 (now renamed EC 1/4 following the creation of the 4th Combat Wing at BA113), were deployed to H4 or Prince Hassan Air Base, in Jordan, from where they conducted hundreds of combat sorties.

During a US, UK and France joint strike on the chemical weapon facilities of the Syrian armed forces in the early hours of 14 April 2018, three Rafale Bs from EC 1/4 together with two Rafale Cs from ETR 3/4 flew from BA113 Saint-Dizier with air-refuelling support provided by C-135FRs, and launched ten SCALP-EG cruise missiles at Syria. One missile fell into the Mediterranean Sea due to technical failure while two hit a weapon storage site in the west of Homs and seven others hit weapon bunkers in the east of the city.

To carry out High Value Air Asset Combat Air Patrol (HAVCAP) and Forward Combat Air Patrol (FORCAP) to protect the E-3F AEW&Cs, C-135FR tankers, Rafale B/Cs and French Navy ships, the French Air Force also had four Mirage 2000-5Fs from EC 1/2 'Cigognes' each armed with two MBDA MICA-EM BVRAAMs, two MICA-IR SRAAMs and three external tanks. The Rafales, which were carrying two SCALP-EGs and three external tanks, were also armed with two MICA-IRs and two MICA-EMs to protect themselves in case of confrontation.

Today, EC 1/4 Gascogne has four escadrilles each with decades of history. They are BR66 'Faucon Egyptien', SAL28 'Eléphant', SPA37 'Charognard' and SPA79 'Tête de Loup'. As of February 2023, emblems from these escadrilles had been painted on the vertical stabilisers of 24 Rafale Bs from the 4th Combat Wing including: 308/4-HA, 310/4-HC, 311/4-HD, 312/4-HF, 314/4-GP, 315/4-HK, 319/4-HN, 320/4-HV, 322/4-HU, 323/4-HT, 326/4-HY, 327/4-HZ, 328/4-IC, 331/4-IF, 333/4-IH, 335/4-IJ, 337/4-IL, 340/4-FG, 341/4-FH, 342/4-FI, 344/4-FK, 347/4-FN, 354/4-FU and 355/4-FV.

For many years the Mirage IV was the main French nuclear strike bomber but towards the end of its career it was used as a recce platform, hence the 'P' at the end of the type designation. 61/CH was one of the last examples operated for long-range reconnaissance by ERS 1/91 Gascogne until its retirement in 2005. It has been in storage at BA113 Saint-Dizier since 30 June 2005. (Babak Taghvaee)

308/4-HA sports the insignia of SPA79 'Tête de Lou' escadrille from EC 1/4 Gascogne on its vertical stabiliser at Orleans in July 2022. (Babak Taghvaee)

312/4-HF, a Rafale B from the 4th Fighter Wing of the FASF, with the insignia of EC 1/4 Gascogne on its vertical stabiliser is armed with a SCALP-EG cruise missile at BA113 Saint-Dizier on 4 October 2019. (Babak Taghvaee)

323/4-HT, a Rafale B from the FASF's 4th Fighter Wing, with the emblem of BR66 Faucon Egyptien escadrille from EC 1/4 Gascogne on its tail, is armed with four GBU-12 LGBs and MICA-IR SRAAMs (on the wing tip launchers) prior to receiving fuel from a KC-135R tanker from the USAF during Operation *Inherent Resolve* in Iraq on 1 July 2017. (SSgt Michael Battles / US Air Force)

326/4-HY is a Rafale B from the 4th Fighter Wing carrying the insignia of the BR66 Faucon Egyptien escadrille from the EC 1/4 Gascogne on its vertical stabiliser. Here it can be seen in Orange in October 2021. (Babak Taghvaee)

328/4-IC, a Rafale B, usually operated by the EC 1/4 Gascogne. It is equipped with a Reco NG reconnaissance pod during exercise Volfa-2022 at BA118 Mont-de-Marsan in October 2022. (Babak Taghvaee)

344/4-FK is a Rafale B from the 4th Fighter Wing of the FASF, which carries the emblem of SPA37 'Charognard' escadrille from EC 1/4 Gascogne on its vertical stabiliser. It is photographed at Orleans in July 2021. (Babak Taghvaee)

This image, taken on 1 July 2017, shows a Rafale B from EC 1/4 Gascogne with s/n 322 and 4-HU code prior to receiving fuel from a USAF KC-135R tanker over Iraq during Opération *Chammal*. The aircraft has the insignia of SPA79 'Tête de Loup' escadrille from EC 1/4 Gascogne on its vertical stabiliser. (SSgt Michael Battles / US Air Force)

Rafale B/Cs of ETR 3/4 Aquitaine: 2010 to today

Today, French Rafale pilots including those from the Navy pass conversion or transition training in the Escadron de Transformation Rafale (ETR) 3/4 Aquitaine from the FASF at BA113 Saint-Dizier. As of February 2023, four Rafale Cs with s/n 136, 139, 140 and 147 and nine Rafale Ms with s/n 303, 313, 317, 325, 339, 346, 349, 350 and 356 had the insignias of the squadron's three escadrilles painted on their vertical tails. These aircraft were mostly used for training alongside four French Navy Rafale Ms with s/n 8, 28, 29 and 40. The 3B3 'Hibou' and 2.GB I/25 'Bison' escadrilles operate all three types while SPA160 'Diable Rouge' escadrille only operates Rafale Bs.

Aquitaine squadron has a rich history dating back to 1958. It was formed as the Centre of Bombardment Instruction 328 (Centre d'Instruction du Bombardement 328) at Cognac. Originally it had three squadrons; the first was equipped with B-26 Invader bombers, the second operated CM-170 Magister training aircraft, and the third operated SO-4050 Vautour IIA and Vautour IIB bombers. On 12 December 1958, the centre became the 92nd Wing and an operator of Vautour bombers only.

Aquitaine's squadrons included Bomber Squadron 2/92. A letter dated 26 May 1959 signed by Gal Leclere, commander of Bomber Command of the French Air Force, authorised 2/92 Squadron to take over the custody of the traditions, insignia and pennants of Bomber Group 1/25 Tunisie (Tunisia), and to bear the name 'Bombardment Squadron 2/92 Aquitaine'.

The 92nd Wing became the 92e Escadre de Bombardement (92nd Bomber Wing) on 1 May 1964, with EB 1/92 Bourgogne and EB 2/92 Aquitaine attached to the unit. The EB 2/92 was dissolved on 1 September 1974. Nevertheless, the 92nd Wing was maintained, bringing together the last Vautour II B to which was added the Vautour II N that the 30th Fighter Wing operated before its transformation into a Mirage F1-type squadron.

When the 92nd Bomber Wing was dissolved on 1 September 1978, the traditions including the name of Aquitaine were taken over by the CIFAS 328 (which was equipped with Mirage IV A) and then by the CITAC 339 Aquitaine from 2001 to 2006.

CITAC 339 operated Jaguar, Alphajet and Mystère/Falcon 20SNA. Its Falcon 20s were 483 and 451, which had Mirage 2000N's RDY radar and its navigator cockpit for training purposes. Both of the Falcon 20SNAs with s/n 483 and 451 were retired in 2006 effectively closing the centre on 30 June 2006. The CITAC was replaced by the Centre de Formation des Crews de Mirage 2000 N (CFEN) integrated into the EC 2/4 La Fayette.

On 27 June 2006, Escadron de Chasse 1/7 Provence, the first French Air Force squadron to operate the Dassault Rafale B combat-trainers, attained full operational capability at Air Base Saint-Dizier 113. For four years, the EC 1/7 Provence trained Rafale pilots until this task was transferred to ETR 2/92 Aquitaine after its formation at BA113 on 1 October 2010. On 26 August 2015, the ETR 2/92 was attached to the 4th Combat Wing and a year later, on 1 September 2016, it was redesignated ETR 3/4.

The ETR 2/93 was formed with two escadrilles, which were 4B3 'Owl' and 1/25(2) 'Bison'. After the redesignation of the squadron into ETR 3/4, the SPA 160 'Red Devil' was also added in 2016. The first two operated all three types of the Rafale while the last escadrille only operated Rafale Bs for weapon system operator (WSO) training.

Since its formation in 2010, the Rafale Transition Squadron has trained almost 200 pilots and tens of weapon system operators. Originally it had 12 aircraft but after formation of the third escadrille, the number of aircraft reached 18. The squadron currently operates ten Rafale Bs, four Rafale Cs and four Rafale Ms. The Naval Rafale Ms are operated by ten technicians and engineers as well as two instructor pilots from Navy Aviation (Aéronavale).

The main mission of the Rafale Transformation Squadron (ETR) is to train young pilots and navigators fresh out of school into experienced Rafale crews. It also trains French Rafale pilots and navigators, including those in the French Navy, as well as foreign pilots. The squadron is responsible for basic pilot flight training and WSO basic weapons training on Rafale. The Rafale crew training includes ten simulator sessions.

To carry out this training, the squadron relies on experienced air personnel, including flight simulator instructors. They have expertise flying the Rafale, and know the plane in the smallest detail. Trainees simulate aircrew missions on simulators and then learn to use the Rafale. They follow pilots and navigators on their first simulators before they go on a real flight. The difficulty of simulator missions is increased by including technical failures. After that, the trainees perform their training in the presence of an instructor pilot in the front or back seat of their aircraft.

Another series of missions performed by ETR 3/4 is to train crews already in the squadron, who must practise on a simulator several times a year to learn how to deal with incidents caused by technical failures. Some qualifications require the passing of simulator missions.

The airmen of this unit may be required to go on external operations abroad (*Chammal, Barkhane, Amber, Herodotus* and Baltic Air policing) or take operational domestic missions. The other task of the ETR 3/4 is to host the Rafale Solo Display (RSD).

For years the FASF student pilots passed training in the Aquitaine squadron after successfully completing their basic, primary and undergraduate training on Cirrus SR20/22s, Grob G-120A-Fs and then Alpha Jet advanced jet trainers. Since 2022, with the removal of Alpha Jet Es from training service, the PC-21 and PC-21-NG turboprop training aircraft are in use for cadet advanced training before they enter the ETR 3/4 for final transition training on Rafale Bs and then Rafale Cs. The cost of pilot training up to graduation from ETR 3/4 is almost 2 million Euro. In addition to training French pilots, the ETR 3/4 also trained Egyptian, Greek, Indian and Qatari Rafale instructor pilots between 2016 and 2021.

313/4-HI is one of nine Rafale Bs in use by ETR E/4 Aquitaine of the FASF, which has the insignia of 2.GB I/25 'Bison' escadrille on the left side of its vertical stabiliser. It can be seen at Orange air base in October 2022. (Babak Taghvaee)

346/4-FM is a Rafale B in use with the ETR 3/4 Aquitaine. The aircraft has the insignia of SPA160 'Diable Rouge' on the left side of its vertical stabiliser. It is landing at Orleans in July 2022. (Babak Taghvaee)

346/4-FM is a Rafale B from ETR 3/4 Aquitaine. Here, it is equipped with a Targeting Long-range Identification Optronic System (TALIOS) pod. It is equipped with top-down and bottom-up datalinks, and covers the entire range of missions, from intelligence to acquiring and pursuing targets. (Babak Taghvaee)

A Rafale C from the FASF with s/n 109 and 4-IM code in July 2021. The aircraft was later transferred to the 30th Combat Wing and received the 30-IM code in October 2021. (Babak Taghvaee)

This Rafale C with s/n 109 was used by the Rafale Solo Display Team from ETR 3/4 Aquitaine in 2019. The aircraft logged many flying hours in the 4th Fighter Wing before being transferred to the 30th Fighter Wing at BA118 Mont-de-Marsan in October 2021. (Babak Taghvaee)

139/4-GR is one of four Rafale Cs from ETR 3/4 Aquitaine. It was used for the Rafale Solo Display team in 2021. (Babak Taghvaee)

136/4-GO is one of four Rafale Cs from ETR 3/4 Aquitaine. It was used by the Rafale Solo Display Team in 2022. (Babak Taghvaee)

During Opération *Serval*, EC 1/7 Provence personnel were involved and flew several Rafale B/Cs including this example with s/n 317 and 4-HO code, although the aircraft belonged to ETR 3/4 Aquitaine. It is seen prior to receiving fuel from a USAF KC-135R tanker on 17 March 2013. (Capt Jason Smith/US Air Force)

A Rafale B from ETR 3/4 Aquitaine in use with EC 1/7 Provence and armed with four GBU-12 LGBs before receiving fuel from a KC-135R from the USAF's 100th ARW during Opération *Serval* in Mali on 23 April 2013. (1st Lt Christopher Mesnard/US Air Force)

Rafale B/Cs of EC 3/30 Lorriane: 2010 to today

EC 3/30 Lorraine is currently one of two fighter units of the FASF operating Rafale C single-seater multi-role fighter jets at BA118 Mont-de-Marsan. Currently, 29 Rafale Cs and five Rafale Bs are in service with the 30th Combat Wing of the FASF. Among them, one Rafale C and three Rafale Bs are in use with CAEM's ECE 1/30 for test purposes, leaving two Rafale Bs and 28 Rafale Cs for use with the two fighter units of the wing which are RC (Fighter Regiment) 2/30 Normandie Niemen and EC (Fighter Squadron) 3/30 Lorraine.

As of February 2023, 18 Rafale Cs and two Rafale Bs from the 30th Combat Wing had the insignias from SPA38 'Chardon Lorrain', SAL56 'Scarabée' and SPA162 'Tête de tigre' escadrilles from EC 3/30 painted on their tails. The Rafale Bs were 324/30-HW and 359 while the Rafale Cs were 104/30-HH, 106/30-HG, 108/30-HS, 110/30-IN, 115/30-IT, 117/30-IV, 119/30-IX, 121/30-IZ, 124/30-GC, 128/30-GG, 134/30-GM, 135/30-GN, 142/30-GU, 144/30-GW, 145/30-GX and 146/30-GY.

Created in September 1940 as No. 1 Bombardment Group at the instigation of General de Gaulle, it was named 'Lorraine' a year later. It was first deployed on the Mediterranean front, in Libya and then in Syria, and finally in Great Britain in autumn 1942 following the occupation of France. While there, it became the 342nd squadron of the Royal Air Force and specialised in night bombing.

On 6 June 1944, in the early morning, the unit wrote one of its most heroic pages of history, taking part in Operation *Smoke Screen* alongside the RAF's 88th Squadron. At a few feet in altitude, the Douglas Boston (A-20 Havoc) from Lorraine successfully dropped a thick screen of smoke in front of the Normandy beaches, thus protecting the allied fleet, which was about to land. At the end of D-Day, the group took part in the liberation of France and the allied territories. On 2 May 1945, at the end of its last mission, the group carried out 3,000 sorties and dropped 2,500 tons of bombs. During World War Two 127 of its pilots, navigators and gunners lost their lives.

After the war, the Lorraine unit had its designation changed following the change in type of its aircraft. It operated SNCASO SO-4050 Vulture IINs from 1957 and 1973. In that period, it was a Fighter Squadron (1953–62) and All-Weather Fighter Squadron (1962–73). After the beginning of Mirage F1C operations from June 1973 until the withdrawal of the type from service on 25 June 2003, the unit was a fighter squadron (EC3/30 from 1973 to 1994 and EC3/33 from 1994 to 2005). The unit operated Mirage F1CT multi-role fighter jets and Mirage F1Bs between 2003 and 2005. The unit, designated as EC 3/30 again, was disbanded in 2005.

Lorraine was reborn in 2011 at the Al Dhafra base in the United Arab Emirates. Ideally positioned, it had been participating in Opération *Chammal* since September 2014. It then operated on a mixed fleet composed of Mirage 2000-5s and Rafales and finally on Rafales exclusively. In 2016, the squadron replaced the 1/7 Provence Fighter Squadron and settled permanently in the BA118 Mont-de-Marsan, Landes region with single-seater Rafales exclusively and since then, the squadron has participated in various operations in Africa.

In the first months after Russia's invasion of Ukraine, which began on 24 February 2022, the squadron directly from BA118 supported by Boeing C-135FR and Airbus A330-243MRTT tankers from the FASF performed six to eight-hour long combat air patrols over Poland and Romania to strengthen the defence of NATO's Eastern fronts. In December 2022, the squadron's crew and personnel were deployed with four Rafale Cs of the 30th Combat Wing to Šiauliai, Lithuania, for NATO Baltic Air Policing missions until March 2023. A similar mission was conducted by RC 2/30 Normandie-Niemen using four Rafale Cs, which were deployed to Malbork, Poland, from May to September 2014.

This historic image, taken on 31 May 1986, shows two Mirage F1Cs from the 30th Fighter Wing from BA 112 Reims-Champagne. They are carrying Matra R530 BVRAAMs under their wings, and R550 Magic-I SRAAMs. The nearest Mirage F1C, with code 30-MO, was based at EC 2/30 'Normandie-Niemen', while the second, with code 30-FO, was based at EC 3/30 Lorraine. (US Defence Imagery)

328/104-IC was a Rafale B from the French Air Force's EC 3/30 Lorraine, based in BA 104 Abu-Dhabi until 2017. It, together with a Rafale C of the squadron, was sent to LIMA 2015 airshow in Langkawi Island, Malaysia, in March 2015. (Babak Taghvaee)

A Rafale C armed with four GBU-12 LGBs is being refuelled by a USAF KC-135R tanker over Iraq during Opération *Chammal* on 8 January 2016. The aircraft was being flown by a pilot from EC 3/30 Lorraine, which later moved from Abu-Dhabi to Mont-de-Marsan, France. (Tech Sgt Nathan Lipscomb / US Air Force)

Until late-2016, it was the responsibility of the EC 3/30 Lorraine based in Abu-Dhabi to carry out French airstrikes against Daesh during Opération *Chammal*. 119/30-IX was one of that squadron's aircraft and can be seen armed with four SBU-54 AASMs over Iraq on 17 October 2016. (SSgt Douglas Ellis / US Air Force)

A French Air Force Rafale from EC 3/30 Lorraine is armed with four SBU-54 AASMs; it is being refuelled over Iraq by a KC-135R from the USAF on 17 October 2016 (SSgt Douglas Ellis/US Air Force)

136 is currently in use with ETR 3/4 Aquitaine with new code 4-GO, but when this Rafale C was photographed in Orange in October 2021, it was in use with EC 3/30 Lorraine of the 30th Fighter Wing. It had the insignia of SPA38 'Chardon Lorrainne' escadrille on its vertical stabiliser. (Babak Taghvaee)

119/30-IX is a Rafale C carrying the insignia of EC 3/30 Lorraine at BA118 Mont-de-Marsan. It can be seen during exercise Volfa-2022 in October 2022. (Babak Taghvaee)

142/30-GU is a Rafale C regularly in use with EC 3/30 Lorraine. It carries the insignia of SAL56 'Scarabée' escadrille from EC 3/30 painted on its vertical stabiliser. It is seen during exercise Volfa-2022 in BA118 Mont-de-Marsan in October 2022. (Babak Taghvaee)

Rafale Cs of RC 2/30 Normandie-Niemen: 2011 to today

Since 25 August 2011, the Fighter Regiment 2/30 'Normandie-Niemen' has operated Rafale C fighter jets. On 28 June 2012, the regiment gained fully operational capability and since then, it has been involved in a number of operations ranging from NATO's air-policing missions over Eastern Europe and airstrikes in Iraq and Syria. The regiment has three escadrilles, which are SPA97 'Fanion aux Hermines', SPA93 'Canard Col Vert' and SPA91 'Aigle à tête de mort', each with a rich history.

Despite the fact that RC 2/30 based at Mont-de-Marsan, is the major operator of Rafale Cs in the 30th Combat Wing, as of February 2023, only 15 Rafale Cs had emblems and insignias of that regiment's escadrilles painted on their vertical stabilisers. They were 102/30-EF, 105/30-HE, 109/30-IM, 114/30-IS, 116/30-IU, 125/30-GD, 126/30-GE, 129/30-GH, 131/30-GJ and 133/30-GL. These aircraft were shared with EC 3/30. In addition to them, these two fighter units from the 30th Combat Wing often borrowed Rafale Cs from BA113 based ETR 3/4 for exercises and special events.

The history of the regiment dates back to 1 September 1942 when it was formed as Fighter Group 3 'Normandie' at Rayak, Lebanon, on the order of General Martial Valin, commander of the Free French Air Force. The squadron was created a year after negotiations between General de Gaulle and representatives from the USSR and Great Britain for help provided to the Free French Air Force with combat aircraft and pilots. Less than a month after its formation, 58 personnel of the newly formed group flew to the USSR via Iraq and Iran and reached Ivanovo on December 2.

In the USSR, they began training in a Soviet fighter training centre located 250km (150 miles) northeast of Moscow. Training began on Yakovlev Yak-1 and Yak-7 Soviet-made piston-engined fighter aircraft. In February 1943, Major Pouliquen was assigned to the French military mission in Moscow and Jean Tulasne was appointed as commander of the fighter group.

After it became operational, the fighter group, comprising French and Russian personnel, was deployed to the front during World War Two from 22 March 1943. They fought alongside the 18th Guards Regiment of the USSR Air Force and created strong bonds between the two units. The Group received its first Yak-9 in September 1943. During the first campaign in which the group was involved, the squadron lost 21 of its pilots leaving only four remaining. The group was stationed in Tula, south of Moscow, in November 1943.

During the campaign in 1944, the unit, which had become a regiment with four escadrilles, scored 77 confirmed victories against the Luftwaffe. In May 1944, the regiment supported the ground offensive of the Red Army against the Reich troops in Belarus. In July, the unit was deployed to Lithuania and carried out a similar mission in support of Soviet forces, which crossed the Niemen river. It was awarded the designation of Niemen Regiment by Marshal Stalin. By 1 August 1944, all of its Yak-3s were replaced by more modern Piston-engined Yak-9s. With these aircraft, the Normandie-Niemen regiment scored 26 victories against the Luftwaffe during the battle in East Prussia in October 1944.

In December 1944, the regiment was prepared for its third campaign during World War Two during which it was directly involved in fierce air combat against the Luftwaffe in Germany. In April 1945, the regiment, which was formed of French and Russian pilots and technicians, participated in the last battle against the Luftwaffe using Yak-3s recently arrived through Iran. A month later, on 12 May, its pilots returned to Moscow and received rewards from Stalin. On 20 June 1945, 37 Yak-9s from the regiment landed in Le Bourget airfield, Paris.

After the war, the regiment flew with Soviet Yak-3s and NC900s (FW-190s assembled in France). In April 1947, the regiment moved to Rabat-Sale air base in Morocco and was equipped with the De Havilland Mosquito and then US-built P-47 Thunderbolts. In November of that year, the unit was attached to the newly formed 6th Fighting Wing and was renamed Fighter Group 2/6. Two years later, the Group received Bell P-63 King Cobra piston-engined fighters as a replacement for its Mosquito bombers. Then it left for Indochina and carried out 4,977 missions and over 6,900 flying hours until May 1951.

The unit later participated in the Algerian war with its P-47s. Vautour II N two-seater multi-role fighter jets arrived in 1958 and changed the designation of the unit to All-Weather Fighter Squadron 2/6. The squadron left Algeria with a total of 1,809 missions and 3,882 flight hours and joined the Orange base in France in 1962.

In January 1967, the unit was based in Reims and four years later, conversion of the squadron to Mirage F1Cs began, fully replacing the Vautour II Ns in 1974. After that, the squadron's designation was changed to Fighter Squadron. The unit's Mirage F1s were mostly specialised for air defence missions. After delivery of multi-role F1CTs, the squadron took part in various overseas operations, such as Turquoise in Rwanda and Crecerelle in Bosnia in 1994; Almandin II in the Central African Republic and Epervier in Chad in 1995; Trident in 1999; Artemis-Mamba in the Democratic Republic of Congo in 2003; and several other operations in the Central African Republic in 2006 and 2007.

On 27 June 2008, the Fighter Group 1/30 'Alsace' was disbanded and its aircraft were absorbed by the Normandie-Niemen unit, which had become Fighter Regiment 1/30. As a result, it had 18 Mirage F1CTs and seven Mirage F1Bs with 203 personnel to carry out three types of missions including air defence of the French mainland, maintaining a permanent detachment in Chad, and training young pilots on the Mirage F1Bs. The regiment was temporarily disbanded on 3 July 2009.

In 2010, the transition began for some of the former Mirage F1 pilots to the Rafale C alongside preparation of its groundcrew for a move to BA118 Mont-de-Marsan. On 22 August 2011, the unit, now named Fighter Squadron (EC) 2/30, arrived at Mont-de-Marsan with eight pilots, three with past experience on Rafale Cs in the EC 1/7, two ex-Mirage F1CT pilots, one ex-Mirage 2000-5 pilot, one Mirage 2000D pilot and a young pilot. A year later, with the completion of the training of more pilots and delivery of more Rafale Cs, the squadron became fully operational at BA118 on 28 June 2012. From September 2012, the squadron, alongside EC 1/7, and EC 1/91, was certified for overseas operational duties.

Since 2012, the squadron, which is now a regiment again, has lost its original escadrilles inherited from the Mirage F1CT era and has now three escadrilles from the World War One era, which are SPA91, SPA93 and SPA97. In addition to its participation in a NATO Baltic Air Policing mission in Poland in 2014, the regiment has participated in four overseas operations, which are *Serval* and *Barkhane* in Africa, *Hamilton* in Syria (against chemical weapon facilities on 14 April 2018) and *Chammal* (from 2016).

In addition to operational deployments to Africa and the Middle East (H4 air base in Jordan), the squadron's Rafale Cs have been involved in operations within Europe. They performed tens of combat air patrols over the Eastern fronts of NATO, particularly Poland and Romania following Russia's invasion of Ukraine in 2022. Also, three pilots and several technicians of the regiment were involved in a NATO Baltic Air Policing mission in Lithuania between December 2022 and March 2023. That mission also involved EC 3/30 Lorraine. The squadron, together with RC 2/30 Normandie-Niemen, operated four Rafale Cs of the 30th Combat Wing during that mission.

On the 80th anniversary of the formation of RC 2/30 Normandie-Niemen, this Rafale C with s/n 125 and 30-GD code received this special paint scheme in 2022. It is landing at BA118 Mont-de-Marsan in October 2022. (Babak Taghvaee)

Taken during exercise Volfa-2022 on 6 October 2022 at BA118 Mont-de-Marsan are a group of Rafale Cs from EC 2/30 and 3/30 of the FASF. (Babak Taghvaee)

125/30-GD was often flown by the commander of RC 2/30 Normandie-Niemen and because of that, it received a special 80th anniversary paint scheme in 2022. It is taking part in exercise Volfa-2022 in BA118. (Babak Taghvaee)

140/30-GS was a Rafale C from RC 2/30 Normandie-Niemen in 2019 when it was used by the squadron to escort several B-52Hs from the USAF over France during a joint training exercise on 25 October 2019. (Tech Sgt Christopher Ruano / US Air Force)

112/30-IQ was a Rafale C from FASF's 30th Combat Wing and was used by RC 2/30 Normandie Niemen during exercise Iniochos-2021 in Andravida, Greece, in April 2021. (Babak Taghvaee)

121/30-IZ is a Rafale C from FASF's 30th Fighter Wing and has the insignia of RC 2/30 Normandie Niemen on its vertical stabiliser. It is seen during exercise Volfa-2022 at BA118 in October 2022. (Babak Taghvaee)

126/30-GE (nearest aircraft) is a Rafale C from FASF's 30th Fighter Wing carrying the insignia of RC 2/30 Normandie Niemen on its vertical stabiliser. It is taking part in exercise Volfa-2022 at BA118 in October 2022. (Babak Taghvaee)

Rafale Bs of EC 2/4 La Fayette: 2015 to today

EC 2/4 La Fayette is one of three squadrons operating Rafale multi-role fighter jets in BA113 and is one of two qualified for nuclear deterrence as part of the French Strategic Air Forces and nuclear weapon capable Rafale Bs and their ASMP-A nuclear cruise missiles. It is currently formed of three escadrilles, which are SPA81 'Lévrier', SPA96 'Gaulois' and SPA167 'Cigogne de Romanet' as well as a unit named N124 'La Fayette – Tete de Sioux'.

Emblems and insignias of these four units are painted on the vertical stabilisers of 14 Rafale Bs of the 4th Combat Wing. They are: 307/4-IA, 318/4-HM, 321/4-HQ, 332/4-IG, 334/4-II, 336/4-IK, 338/4-IO, 343/4-FJ, 345/4-FL, 351/4-FR, 352/4-FS, 353/4-FT, 357/4-FX and 358/4-FY. This squadron and EC 1/4 share their aircraft with each other.

The history of the La Fayette squadron dates back to 1 May 1944. It was initially made up of fighter groups 2/3 'Dauphiné', 2/5 'La Fayette' and 1/4 'Navarre', which date back to World War One. Fighter Group 3/3 'Ardennes' was associated with the squadron on 31 October 1944 and Fighter Group 1/4 'Navarre' was detached on 7 December1944. The 4th Fighter Squadron, with tireless energy, took part in the war using its P-47 Thunderbolt from Provence for the liberation of France. On 8 May 1945, it recorded more than 10,000 sorties. More than 4,500 tons of bombs were dropped on targets of all types during the war by the squadron.

On 1 July 1947, Fighter Group 2/5 became 2/4 'La Fayette' and participated in the Indochina war with Spitfires Mark IX and logged 8,663 flying hours until November 1948. On its return to Europe, the 4th Fighter Squadron was based in Friedrichshafen, Germany, and started operating P-47Ds until its transformation to Vampire Mark V jet fighters began in October 1949. In 1951, an aerobatic display team was created using Vampires. Later in April 1954, the squadron moved to Bremgarten, where, in July, it began receiving the French-made MD 450 Ouragan, an aircraft on which the Patrouille de France was later equipped.

In May 1957, the squadron transformed into one of the most brilliant fighters of that time with the F-84F Thunderstreak, and four years later, it was based at Luxeuil. In November 1966, when the transformation of the Mirage IIIE began, the F-84Fs of the 4th Fighter Squadron totalled more than 100,000 flight hours. In 1972, the 4th Wing became the first aviation unit of the tactical nuclear forces; its primary mission was all-weather nuclear bombardment with the AN-52 nuclear bombs while its secondary mission was conventional strike and daylight interception.

On 4 October 1986, while preparing for the transformation on the Mirage 2000N, the Mirage IIIEs had flown more than 150,000 hours within the 4th Fighter Squadron in 20 years of operational service. On 30 March 1988, the first Mirage 2000N was delivered to the unit and from July 1 of that same year, they took operational alert on this aircraft equipped with the medium-range air-to-ground missile (ASMP) nuclear cruise missile.

342/125-BA was one of three Mirage 2000Ns of EC 2/4 La Fayette, which was deployed to H4 / Prince Hassan Air Base in Jordan and conducted airstrikes in Iraq and Syria during Opération *Chammal*. **It is pictured over Iraq on 20 August 2015. (SSgt Sandra Welch / US Air Force)**

With the retirement of Mirage IIIEs of the 4th escadrille of the squadron on 1 November 1988, it was the turn of the EC 2/4 'La Fayette', on 1 July 1989, to take part in nuclear deterrence on this new weapon system.

In July 1996, with the end of Mirage IVP's nuclear deterrence missions, Mirage 2000Ns became the only nuclear weapon capable combat aircraft in the French Air Force. On 1 September 2011, EC 3/4 'Limousin', one of two Mirage 2000N operators of the French Strategic Air Forces, was disbanded and its mission was taken up by EC 1/4 Gascogne, which had recently received Rafale Bs capable of using ASMP and ASMP-A nuclear cruise missiles.

Based in BA125 Istres-Le Tube, the EC 2/4 La Fayette had three of its Mirage 2000Ns deployed to H4 air base in Jordan from where they took part in Opération *Chammal* in 2015. In August 2015, the squadron began receiving Rafale Bs, which were based in BA113, to be operated by its ex-Mirage 2000N pilots and WSOs after their graduation from training at ETR 3/4 Aquitaine. Transition of the squadron to Rafale B lasted for three years until it was completed on 29 August 2018. Subsequently, all Mirage 2000Ns were retired that year and the squadron was fully moved to BA113 in Saint-Dizier.

EC 2/4 has participated in a number of overseas missions using Rafale Bs including involvement in Opération *Chammal* from H4/Prince Hassan Air Base in Jordan as well as NATO air-policing missions over NATO's Eastern front with MICA-IR and MICA-EM missile-armed Rafale Bs following Russia's invasion of Ukraine in 2022. These combat air patrols each lasted five to eight hours and were supported by the C-135FRs, KC-135RGs and Airbus A330-243MRTTs of the FASF. They began in June 2022 and lasted until September of the same year.

This Rafale B from FASF's 4th Fighter Wing was operated by EC 2/4 La Fayette to escort a USAF 2nd Bomb Wing B-52H Stratofortress heavy bomber in support of Bomber Task Force Europe 20-1 on 25 October 2019, over France. (Tech Sgt Christopher Ruano / US Air Force)

A formation flight of four Rafale Bs from the 4th Fighter Wing with an Airbus A330-243MRTT tanker, during celebrations for the 55th anniversary of the founding of the French Strategic Air Forces at BA113 Saint-Dizier on 4 October 2019. (Babak Taghvaee)

352/4-FS is a Rafale B often used by the EC 2/4 La Fayette and carries the emblem of SPA96 Gaulois escadrille on its vertical stabiliser. It can be seen during exercise Iniochos-2021 in Andravida, Greece, in April 2021. (Babak Taghvaee)

Dassault Rafale: France's Key to Air-Superiority

352/4-IC is a Rafale B from the 4th Fighter Wing that carries the insignia of EC 2/4 La Fayette on its vertical stabilisers. It can be seen in the main ramp of the FASF's BA113 Saint-Dizier in October 2022. (Babak Taghvaee)

Rafale B/Cs of the French Air and Space Force

351/4-FR is famous in the 4th Fighter Wing for carrying a colourful Insignia from the EC 2/4 La Fayette on its vertical stabiliser in 2022. It is under maintenance in the BA113's maintenance hangar in June 2022. (Babak Taghvaee)

ASMP-A nuclear cruise missile is the most important weapon in the inventory of FASF, which is being used by both EC 1/4 and EC 2/4 for nuclear alert at BA113 Saint-Dizier. (Babak Taghvaee)

Two of these Snecma M88-2 turbofan engines provide significant manoeuvrability for Rafale fighter jets. This engine belonged to 351/4-FR, a Rafale B of the 4th Fighter Wing, usually in use with EC 2/4, in 2022. (Babak Taghvaee)

Chapter 3
Rafales of Egypt, Greece, India and Qatar

Rafale DM/EMs of the Egyptian Air Force: 2015 to today
In 2015, Egypt purchased eight Rafale EM single-seat multi-role fighter jets and 16 Rafale DM two-seater variants of them from France as part of a €5.2–6 billion deal that also covered procurement of 150 MICA-EM/IR air-to-air missiles, 25 SCALP-EG cruise missiles, 300 AASM Hammer precision-guided bombs and 12 TALIOS targeting pods for them. While the contract for sale of the Rafales to Egypt was signed in February 2015, their first three examples, all DM variants with s/n 9251, 9252 and 9253 were flown to Cairo West from Bordeaux on 21 July 2015.

Rafale DM/EMs fighter jets were used to reform the 34th 'Wild Wolves' Squadron of the Egyptian Air Force's 203rd Tactical Fighter Wing, a former operator of Tu-16 heavy bombers between 1965 and 1967. By the end of 2018, 15 more Rafale DMs with s/n 9254 to 9266 and eight Rafale EMs with s/n 9351 to 9359 were delivered. To house the new aircraft at Gebel el Basur air base, the home of the Mirage 2000BM/EM fighter jets of the Egyptian Air Force's 252nd Tactical Fighter Wing, a new maintenance hangar, a new squadron building and six aircraft sheds were constructed in the ramp of the air base.

Rafale DM/EMs were purchased by Egypt to replace the last operational Mirage 5s of the air force, which had been upgraded to SDE2 standard in the early-1990s. With finance from Saudi Arabia, Egypt purchased 54 Mirage 5SDE multi-role fighter jets, six Mirage 5SB combat trainers and six Mirage 5SDR tactical reconnaissance aircraft from France as well as 280 R-530 Magic-I short-range air-to-air missiles between 1973 and 1977. Their deliveries took place between 1973 and 1983. In 1980, 16 Mirage 5SDE2s were ordered with their deliveries taking place in 1983.

During the process of replacing the ageing aircraft of the Egyptian Air Force, decisions were made to buy Mirages from France. In 1983, 16 Mirage 2000EM multi-role fighter jets and four combat trainers were ordered as part of a US$1bn deal with deliveries taking place between 1986 and 1988. To arm them, 20 ATLIS II targeting pods, 120 AS-30L laser-guided air-to-surface missiles, 120 more Matra R550 Magic-I IR-Guided SRAAMs, 80 Super-530D semi-active radar-guided BVRAAMs and 50 ARMAT anti-radiation missiles were purchased with deliveries taking place before the end of 1988.

The Egyptian Air Force continues to operate two Mirage 2000BMs and 16 Mirage 2000EMs in the service of the 82nd Squadron while all of the Mirage 5s were withdrawn from service by 2019. The Egyptian Air Force initially had planned to deliver 24 of them to the Libyan National Air Force, however, this never happened and instead, 36 of them were sold to Pakistan in 2019. They were used as a source of spare parts to keep the large fleet of Mirage 5DD/DSR/PA/DPA2s of the Pakistani Air Force in service.

In April 2019, The Egyptian Air Force lost one of its Rafale EMs in an accident leaving 23 Rafales for the 203rd Tactical Fighter Wing (TFW). Almost half of these Rafales were later assigned to the newly formed 36th 'Lions' Squadron of the 203rd TFW in Habata from 2021. To operate them from the air base in northwest Egypt, renovation work to extend and widen the air base's runways began in 2018. The work was completed at the same time as the construction of 12 new hardened aircraft shelters and a new aircraft ramp in Habata air base.

In 2019, Egypt ordered 24 Su-35SEs, but because of pressure applied by the US government they remained undelivered in 2021. Unable to operate these Russian-made multi-role fighter jets, the Egyptian Air Force bought more Rafales from France. On 3 May 2021, the Egyptian Ministry of Defence confirmed that a contract for 30 Rafale DM/EMs was signed with France. The contract valued at US$4.5bn had 85 per cent finance provided by France through a loan to be paid over at least 10 years.

Today, the Egyptian Air Force operates 296 fighter jets comprising 46 MiG-29M2s, 18 Mirage 2000BM/EMs, 23 Rafale DM/EMs and 209 F-16A/B/C/Ds. Within the past five years, the Egyptian Air Force has used its Rafale EM/DMs in various missions over the west of the country and in eastern Libya. To ensure a high level of combat readiness of the Rafale pilots and WSOs, the 34th and 36th squadrons of 203rd TFW have participated in numerous exercises, including international ones with the French Dassault Rafale B/Cs.

The first two Rafale DMs of the Egyptian Air Force with s/n 9251 and 9252 during the official handover ceremony at Istres on 20 July 2015. (S Rande / Dassault Aviation)

9252 is the second Rafale DM two-seat, multi-role fighter jet ordered by Egypt, seen here prior to delivery in July 2015. (Anthony Pecchi / Dassault Aviation)

9251 and 9252, the first two Rafale DMs of the Egyptian Air Force prior to delivery to Egypt on 16 July 2015. (Anthony Pecchi / Dassault Aviation)

From front to back, 9253, 9252 and 9251, the first three Egyptian Air Force Rafale DMs during a formation flight in France on 16 July 2015. (Anthony Pecchi / Dassault Aviation)

The first two Rafale DMs with s/n 9251 and 9252 are flying next to the pyramids of Giza near Cairo, following delivery on 1 October 2015. (Dassault Aviation)

DM10 became the tenth Rafale DM of the Egyptian Air Force and is rolling out of the final assembly line of the Dassault Aviation facility at Merignac on 5 April 2018. (Sebastien Rande/Dassault Aviation)

DM10 became the tenth Rafale DM of the Egyptian Air Force and is shown in the engine test site of the Dassault Aviation facility at Merignac airport on 5 April 2018. (Sebastien Rande/Dassault Aviation)

DM10 became the tenth Rafale DM of the Egyptian Air Force and is seen freshly painted at the Dassault Aviation facility at Merignac on 22 June 2018. (V Almansa / Dassault Aviation)

DM06, DM08 and DM10, the seventh, eighth and tenth Rafale DM of the Egyptian Air Force respectively, can be seen at Dassault's test facility in Istres in September 2018. (V Almansa / Dassault Aviation)

Rafale DQ/EQs of Qatar Emiri Air Force: 2019 to today

On 30 April 2015, Dassault Aviation announced that the Qatari government had made a decision to acquire 24 Dassault Rafales. Subsequently, a €6.7 billion deal was finalised on 4 May 2015, for the procurement of 18 single-seat Rafale EQs and six two-seat Rafale DQs. The contract included spare parts and maintenance support as well as pilot training, delivery of weapons and other equipment for the aircraft.

For use on the Rafales, 150 MICA-IR SRAAMs, 150 MICA-EM BVRAAMs, 160 Meteor BVRAAMs, 300 AASM Hammer precision-guided bombs, 60 AM.39 Block.2 Mod.2 anti-ship missiles, 140 SCALP-EG cruise missiles, Israeli made Targo-II flight helmets with mounted sights (from Elbit Systems) and Sniper targeting pods were ordered with their deliveries taking place by the end of 2020.

In the presence of the President of the French Republic, Emmanuel Macron and the Sheikh of Qatar, Tamim bin Hamad Al Thani, the Qatar Armed Forces and Dassault Aviation signed an agreement on future co-operation and the exercise of an option for 12 Rafales at Saint-Cloud on 7 December 2017. The exercise of the option for the purchase of 12 additional Rafales, including three DQ (two-seat) variants, came into effect on 27 March 2018.

The first Rafale DM of Qatar's order with c/n DQ01, which later received s/n QA201, logged its first flight from Dassault's production facility at Bordeaux to Dassault's test facilities at Istres on 28 June 2016. A year later, the first single-seat variant with c/n EQ01, which later became QA210, logged its first flight on 27 March 2017, followed by the second copy (EQ02) on 13 April of that year. Two years later, on 6 February 2019, during a ceremony at the Bordeaux-Merignac facility of Dassault Aviation, the first Rafale DQ of Qatar was officially delivered.

Rafale was not the first French-made fighter jet of the Qatari Air Force; that Air Force had operated 12 Mirage F1EDA single-seat multi-role fighter jets and two F1DDA combat-trainers from 1983 until 1994. One F1DDA was lost in 1987 while a F1EDA was lost in February 1991, both in accidents. As a replacement for the lost F1DDA, another two-seat aircraft was ordered in 1987 with its delivery taking place in 1992. Only two years after that, Qatar sold all of its Mirage F1s except the F1DDA to Spain, and that country used them as a source of spare parts for its own Mirage F1s. As a replacement for the Mirage F1s, Qatar procured nine Mirage 2000-5EDA multi-role fighter jets and three Mirage 2000-5DDA combat trainers as a part of a contract that was finalised in 1994.

The Mirage 2000 deliveries took place between 1997 and 1999. At the same time, 50 Apache Black Pearl anti-runway cruise missiles, 100 MICA-EM BVRAAMs and 96 Matra R550 Magic-II IR guided SRAAMs were received to be used on these Mirage 2000s. In addition to these, 90 other Magic-IIs have been available since 1988. They were procured for use on the Mirage F1DDA/EDAs.

The Mirage 2000s were operated by the 7th Air Superiority Squadron of the 1st Fighter Wing at Doha until 2021 when they were retired from service after the 1st Squadron of the Qatari Air Force named Al Adiyat (The War Horses) in the service of the 6th Flying Wing of the Air Force in Tamim air base became fully operational. In addition to nine Rafale DQs and 27 Rafale EQs, the Qatar Emiri Air Force also had 24 airworthy Boeing F-15QA Ababil strike fighters, six Eurofighter EF-2000 Typhoon multi-role fighter jets and two of their combat trainers in service as of February 2023.

Procurement of these fighter jets from the United States, United Kingdom and France by the government of Qatar had political value for the Qatari government, which was faced with political and economic sanctions by its Arab neighbours due to its support of the Muslim Brotherhood and its attempts to overthrow secular governments such as that in Egypt.

From 2020, Qatari Rafales have participated in joint training and exercises with the USAF that have included inflight refuelling training from KC-135R/T tankers based in Al-Udeid Air Base. They also participated in exercise Epic Skies IV in December 2020 in which RAF Typhoon FGR4s participated.

In 2021, four Rafale EQ/DQs participated in exercise Anatolian Eagle 2021 with the Turkish Air Force from Konya air base from June 21 to July 2.

On 18 December 2021, several Rafale DQ/EQs participated in Qatar's National Day Parade during which they were armed with MICA-IR, MICA-EM, Meteor and SCALP EG missiles. One of the Rafale EQs also carried an inflight refuelling pod for simulation of buddy refuelling to a second Rafale EQ during the parade over Doha.

Above: A Rafale EQ and a Rafale DQ of the Qatar Emiri Air Force in the final assembly line of Dassault's Aviation facility in Mergnac in January 2019. (Sebastien Rande / Dassault Aviation)

Right: QA202, a Rafale DQ of the Qatar Emiri Air Force during the official handover ceremony at Dasssault's Merignac facility on 6 February 2019. (Sebastien Rande / Dassault Aviation)

QA217, a Rafale EQ and QA203, a Rafale DQ, of the Qatar Emiri Air Force during a formation flight near Bordeaux prior to delivery in 2019. (Anthony Pecchi / Dassault Aviation)

QA217, a Rafale EQ and QA203, a Rafale DQ, of the Qatar Emiri Air Force during a formation flight near Bordeaux prior to delivery in 2019. (Anthony Pecchi / Dassault Aviation)

The first inflight refuelling of a Qatari aircraft from a USAF tanker took place on 28 December 2020 when this image was taken. This Rafale DQ with s/n QA204 (front) and the Rafale EQ with s/n QA223 (back) received fuel from the USAFs KC-135R. (SSgt Trevor T McBride / US Air Force)

A Rafale DQ of the Qatar Emiri Air Force receiving fuel from a USAF KC-135R tanker during a training mission on 29 December 2020. (Senior Airman Roslyn Ward / US Air Force)

QA216, a Rafale EQ of the Qatar Emiri Air Force is receiving fuel from a USAF KC-135R tanker during a training mission on 31 December 2020. (SSgt Sean Carnes / US Air Force)

Five Rafale EQs and one Rafale DQ of the Qatar Emiri Air Force are flying in formation behind a USAF KC-135R tanker prior to receiving fuel from it during a training mission on 31 December 2020. (SSgt Sean Carnes / US Air Force)

Rafale DH/EHs of Indian Air Force: 2020 to today

In 2016, the government of India placed an order for 36 Dassault Rafale multi-role fighter jets, their spare parts and weapons with a total value of €7.87 billion; 50 per cent offsets included 20 per cent of component production in India. Of this, €5.2 billion was for 24 Rafale EH single-seaters and eight Rafale DH two-seaters, €1.8 billion for the spare parts and €710 million for their armaments comprising 150 MICA-RF BVRAAMs and MICA-IR SRAAMs, 170 SCALP-EG cruise missiles and 300 AASM Hammer precision guided bombs, with deliveries taking place between 2020 and 2022.

India's Rafale programme dates back to 2001 when the country launched a medium multi-role combat aircraft (MMRCA) programme. Established with an almost 20-year timeline, its remit was to obtain 126 combat aircraft to replace its ageing MiG-21 light fighter jets including MiG-21bis versions, which had been upgraded to MiG-21-93 standard. In August 2007, several competitors including Dassault Aviation submitted their offers and, in July 2009, the evaluation of Rafale, Typhoon, F-16C/D, F/A-18E/F, MiG-35 and JAS-39 Gripen began and lasted until April 2010.

The Typhoon and Rafale led the first series of evaluations in April 2011. A year later in January 2012, Dassault began exclusive negotiations with the Indian government offering under-licence assembly and production of 108 out of the 126 aircraft in India. In March 2014, the technology transfer negotiations began with Hindustan Aeronautic Ltd (HAL). Later, on 30 July 2015, India terminated the MMRCA project. On 25 January 2016, a political agreement for the procurement of 36 Rafales was signed. Later, on 23 September 2016, a contract for the procurement of the Rafales was signed valued at €7.87 billion.

In August 2018, the first Rafale Indian order, a 'DH' two-seat variant, logged its first flight in Bordeaux. The aircraft with c/n RB008 was used for system integration tests requested by India at the flight test centre in Istres-Le Tube.

Training the first Indian pilots began from October 2019 and lasted until March 2021 at the Bordeaux-Merignac airport. Most of these pilots were former Indian Air Force Mirage 2000H pilots. In September 2019, the Indian Air Force reactivated its Squadron 17 named 'Golden Arrows' at Ambala Air Base (Haryana) to operate the aircraft. By the beginning of 2020 all of its Rafale DHs were operational in France and the first batch were flown to India on 27 July 2020. They officially entered service with the Indian Air Force on 10 September 2020 and participated in celebrations for the 88th anniversary of the foundation of the Indian Air Force in October 2020.

On 30 October 2020, two Rafale EHs with c/n BS002 and BS005 and one two-seat Rafale DH with c/n RB003 were delivered. On 27 January 2021, three more Rafales flew to Ambala air base, India, from France, followed by three on 26 March and three on 21 April 2021. Nine more Rafales were delivered on 5 May, 21 May and 16 July 2021

On the 75th anniversary of India's independence, one Rafale DH and 15 Rafale EHs from the Indian Air Force taxied in close proximity in an elephant walk along with Jaguar IS/IT fighter jets of the 5th and 14th squadrons at Ambala Air Base. In December 2022, the last Indian Rafale flew from France. Rafale DH with c/n RB008 had been used for test flights at the test centre of Dassault Aviation in Istres. Because of the large increase in Rafale DH/EHs now in service in India, a second squadron was established. Known as 101 'Falcons' Squadron of 16 Wing, it was based at Jalpaguiri/Hashimara Air Base, located in the east of the country.

The Rafale is not the only French-made combat aircraft owned by India. Its air force has operated Mirage 2000H multi-role fighter jets and Mirage 2000TH combat trainers since 1985. Back in 1982, India ordered 36 Mirage 2000Hs and four Mirage 2000THs as well as 200 AS-30L laser-guided air-to-surface missiles, 500 Matra R550 Magic-II IR-guided SRAAMs and 200 Super-530D BVRAAMs for use on them. They were delivered in 1985 and 1986. An additional order was placed for six more Mirage 2000Hs and three more Mirage 2000THs in 1986 with their deliveries taking place in 1987 and 1988.

To give precision strike capability to its Mirage 2000s, India purchased ten ATLIS II targeting pods and 200 BGL-1000 precision guided bombs for use on the Mirage 2000H/THs. Later in 2000, a US$312–353m order was placed for four additional Mirage 2000Hs and six Mirage 2000THs and finally in 2021, a €27m order was placed for 13 secondhand Mirage 2000C/Bs rebuilt into H/TH standard. In addition to them, 11 more secondhand Mirage 2000Cs were ordered, to be used as a source of spare parts.

In 2011, a deal was finalised with Dassault Aviation with a total price US$2.3–2.6bn (US$593m offsets) for modernisation of the 49 Mirage 2000H/THs into Mirage 2000-5 standard. Two aircraft were upgraded in France while the modernisation work of the rest will take place at HAL facility in India up until 2025. To arm these upgraded aircraft known as Mirage 2000HI/THIs as well as those still not upgraded, 493 MICA-EM/IR air-to-air missiles were ordered with a total value of €950m (offsets 30 per cent) in 2012 with their deliveries taking place between 2014 and 2021.

Like the Egyptian Air Force, the Indian Air Force will operate both Dassault Rafale and Mirage 2000-5s for decades while in Qatar and Greece, Rafales have already replaced the Mirage 2000-5s (Qatar) or are in the process of doing so (Greece).

RB002, the second Indian Air Force Rafale during a flight in France on 14 June 2018. (G Gosset / Dassault Aviation)

The official handover ceremony of India's first Rafale DH with s/n RB001 at Dassault's Merignac facility in the presence of Indian and French Defence Ministers on 8 October 2019. (V Almansa / Dassault Aviation)

RB005, a Rafale DH, in the final stages of assembly at Dassault's Merignac facility during the official visit of the Indian Defence Minister, Mantri Shri Rajnath Singh, on 8 October 2019. (V Almansa / Dassault Aviation)

RB002, the second Indian Air Force Rafale DH during a flight in France on 14 June 2018. (G Gosset / Dassault Aviation)

BS005, an Indian Air Force Rafale EH is flying in formation with a Mirage 2000HI, a Mirage 2000TH and a Su-30MKI alongside a French Air and Space Force Rafale B during exercise Shikra on 21 January 2021. (French Air and Space Force)

Rafale DG/EGs of Hellenic Air Force: 2021 to today

The 19 January 2022 marked a new chapter in the contemporary history of the Hellenic Air Force's Air Supremacy over the Aegean Sea, when it had its first Rafale DG/EG multi-role fighter jets located at their home base, Tanagra in Greece. The aircraft were delivered to 332 Mira (squadron) less than two years after a contract for their purchase was finalised. They replaced the last Mirage 2000EG SG.3s (Standard Greece 3) and the Mirage 2000BG combat trainers, which were withdrawn from service from 332 Mira from the air force's 114th Combat Wing at Tanagra in December 2021.

On 12 September 2020, the government of Greece announced that it had selected the Rafale multi-role fighter jet to replace its last Mirage 2000BGM/EGMs, which were nearing the end of their lives. The Greek Parliament approved the procurement of 18 Rafales for its air force as part of the France-Greece strategic partnership following the rise in threats from Turkey.

In September 2020, the Hellenic Air Force had 32 Mirage 2000s in service with 114 Combat Wing at Tanagra Air Base. Twenty four of them were Mirage 2000-5BG/EGs with RDY-2, while the other eight were Mirage 2000BGM/EGMs. The 332 Mira had ten more Mirage 2000EGMs, which had been withdrawn from service and were kept in storage. The 18 new Rafale fighter jets would take their place from 2022.

On 25 January 2021 the French Minister of Defence, Florence Parly, travelled to Greece to meet the Greek Prime Minister, the Defence Minister and the Chief of the Air Force. On that day, the order for the fighter aircraft was officially placed. Twelve were secondhand and supplied from the inventory of the French Air and Space Force while the other six were to be newly built. Later, on 22 March 2022, an additional order for six more Rafale DG/EGs was placed with their deliveries scheduled to take place in 2024.

Starting from March 2021, the French Air Force 4th Fighter Wing at Saint-Dizier and 30th Fighter Wing at Mont-de-Marsan each prepared one Rafale B and two Rafale Cs from their inventory for delivery to the Hellenic Air Force. These were first delivered to Dassault Aviation, which upgraded them to F3-R standard prior to their handover to the Hellenic Air Force. The Rafale Bs were renamed as Rafale DGs while the Rafale Cs were renamed as Rafale EGs with the 'E' suffix standing for multi-role.

The first Rafale DG for the Hellenic Air Force with s/n 401 (Rafale B with s/n 305 in the French Air and Space Force) was officially handed over to the Hellenic Air Force at the Dassault Aviation's facility in BA125, Istres on 21 July 2021. The last aircraft of the first batch of six was a Rafale EG with s/n 413, which was delivered in December 2021. It was previously a Rafale C of the French 30th Fighter Wing based at Mont-de-Marsan.

On 19 January 2022, almost a year after finalisation of the first €1.8 billion deal for 12 secondhand Rafales and six brand-new Rafales, the 332 'Hawk' Squadron of the Hellenic Air Force received its first batch of six aircraft comprising two Rafale DGs with s/n 401 and 402, and four Rafale EGs with s/n 410 to 413 during an official ceremony.

The first batch of six Rafale F3-Rs for the Hellenic Air Force were at the Dassault Aviation facility in Bordeaux for use by the Dassault's CTC (Conversion Training Centre) until 14 January 2022 when they flew to Air Base No.125 at Bordeaux where the Dassault Aviation has a test facility. Five days later, they left the base and flew to their new home base at Tanagra.

Later in the last quarter of 2022, the Hellenic Air Force received several brand new (newly constructed) Rafales. There were four Rafale EGs with s/n 450 to 453 and a Rafale DG with s/n 441. A second Rafale DG with s/n 442 was completed and delivered in January 2023. In 2023, six more secondhand Rafale B/Cs from the French Air and Space Force are due to be converted into DG/EG standard and delivered to the Hellenic Air Force along with another batch of six brand new Rafale DG/EGs in 2024. It is expected that Greece will order another 18 to 24 Rafale DG/EGs as replacements for its fleet of Mirage 2000-5BG/EGs currently in service with 331 Mira until 2030.

Greece ordered various weapons and equipment for use on its Dassault Rafale fighter jets including Meteor long-range BVRAAMs. Starting in spring 2023, the Rafale DG/EGs from 332 Mira, which are armed with MICA-IR, MICA-EM and Meteor air-to-air missiles are due to carry out quick reaction alert missions over the Aegean and Mediterranean seas, protecting Greek airspace.

Croatia, Indonesia and the United Arab Emirates are going to operate Dassault Rafale aircraft in the near future. The order for ten secondhand Rafale C F-3Rs and two Rafale B F3-Rs from the French Air and Space Force to Croatia was signed on 25 November 2021, while an order for 42 brand new

Rafale D/E F4s (30 single-seat and 12 double-seat) for Indonesia was signed on 10 February 2022. A government-to-government deal for 80 Rafale D/E F4s for the United Arab Emirates Air Force was signed on 3 December 2021 making the United Arab Emirates the first operator of Rafale F4 standard outside France. Colombia, Iraq and Serbia are three other countries that have also shown an intention to buy 16, 14 and 12 Rafale D/Es respectively, as of February 2023.

401, the first Hellenic Air Force's Rafale DG during a flight over the Mediterranean Sea near Istres on 7 July 2021. (C Cosmo / Dassault Aviation)

401, Greece's first DG-equipped Rafale with a single captive training MICA-IR SRAAM is seen prior to landing at Bordeaux-Merignac airport after a training flight on 14 December 2021. (Babak Taghvaee)

This Rafale B with s/n 305 from the French Air and Space Force is being prepared for delivery to Hellenic Air Force at Dassasult's Istres facility in 2021. (V Almansa / Dassault Aviation)

Greece's first Rafale DG/EGs after the ferry flight from Istres, France, to Tanagra, Greece, for handover to 332 Mira on 19 January 2022. (Babak Taghvaee)

The water salute for s/n 410, the first Rafale EG, after landing in Tanagra, during the handover ceremony to 332 Mira on 19 January 2022. (Babak Taghvaee)

The Hellenic Air Force's Rafale EG with s/n 412 following a ferry flight from Istres, France, to Tanagra, Greece, and 332 Mira on 19 January 2022. (Babak Taghvaee)

402, Greece's second Rafale DG at Tanagra Air Base during the handover ceremony to 332 Mira on 19 January 2022. (Babak Taghvaee)

Other books you might like:

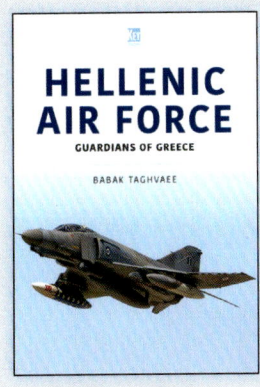
Air Forces Series, Vol. 8

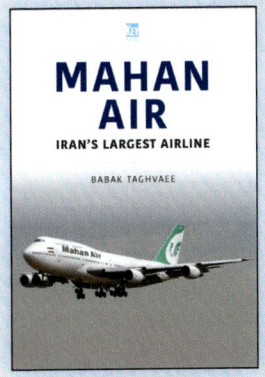
Airlines Series, Vol. 13

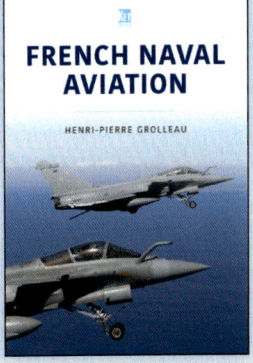
Modern Military Aircraft Series, Vol. 7

Modern Military Aircraft Series, Vol. 5

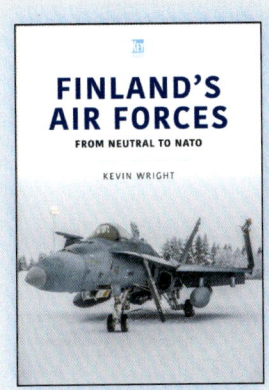
Air Forces Series, Vol. 6

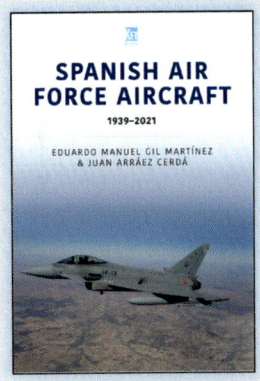
Air Forces Series, Vol. 3

For our full range of titles please visit:
shop.keypublishing.com/books

VIP Book Club

Sign up today and receive
TWO FREE E-BOOKS

Be the first to find out about our forthcoming book releases and receive exclusive offers.

Register now at **keypublishing.com/vip-book-club**

Our VIP Book Club is a 100% spam-free zone, and we will never share your email with anyone else.
You can read our full privacy policy at: privacy.keypublishing.com

410, Greece's first Rafale EG lands at BA105 Evreux on 12 July 2022 just two days before its participation in the Bastille Day Parade over Paris on 14 July 2022. (Babak Taghvaee)

410 and 413 also participated in the Bastille Day Parade over Paris on 14 July 2022. They are flying in the wing of a French Air and Space Force Mirage 2000-5F. (Babak Taghvaee)